Paleo for Beginners

THE GUIDE TO GETTING STARTED

150 recipes   **30**-day meal plan   **10** steps for success

FALL RIVER PRESS

New York

FALL RIVER PRESS

New York

An Imprint of Sterling Publishing Co., Inc.
1166 Avenue of the Americas
New York, NY 10036

ISBN 978-1-4351-5561-9

For information about custom editions, special sales, and premium and
corporate purchases, please contact Sterling Special Sales at
800-805-5489 or specialsales@sterlingpublishing.com.

Manufactured in China

6 8 10 9 7 5

www.sterlingpublishing.com

Photo Credits

Shutterstock:
© Olha Afanasieva: 37; © CGissemann: 145; © Oxana Denezhkina: 40; © B. and E. Dudzinscy: 175;
© Darren K. Fisher: 227; © Yana Gayvoronskaya: 21, 58; © Vania Georgieva: 162; © Jiri Hera: 137;
© Brent Hofacker: 150, 173, 219; © Anna Hoychuk: iv-v, viii, 12, 38, 56, 253; © Iomis: 124;
© Jag_cz: 157; © Kesu: 22, 220; © Robyn Mackenzie: 65; © MamaMiaPL: 117; © Marysckin: 230;
© MShev: 89; © Quanthem: 2, 70, 98, 200; © Joshua Resnick: 207; © Sarsmis: 103;
© Sea Wave: 138; © Timolina: 94; © Zoryanchik: 177; © Magdalena Zurawska: 131

Stockfood
© Klaus Arras: 244; © Rua Castilho: 183; © Michael Cogliantry: 186; © George Crudo: 82;
© La Food/Thomas Dhellemmes – SFGmbH: 258; © A. Hbrkova: 237; © Sarah Hogan: 77;
© Jim Norton: 195; © Yelena Strokin: 134; © Bernhard Winkellmann: 214

Contents

Preface

Has anyone ever told you that you're too smart for your own good?

What they probably meant is that, even though your smarts are impressive, you're in a situation where brains aren't necessarily the answer. As compliments go, this is a bit of a double-edged sword. When you hear it, you might give yourself a pat on the back, and then frantically try to figure out what else you really need in order to succeed, besides smarts.

The food industry is too smart for its own good. After millennia of domesticating plants and animals, building machines that harvest more efficiently, and genetically engineering plumper, hardier crops, no one can say that our accumulated knowledge about food isn't impressively smart. But is it really good for us? Diseases of affluence, like obesity and hypertension, are on the rise. More and more people are finding themselves allergic—or worse—to the very foods that showcase our industrial brainpower, such as the newest forms of wheat. Food is supposed to be good for us. That's its whole purpose. If it has become too smart for our its good, then we should exchange our smarts for a bit more common sense.

If you've heard of the paleo diet, then you've also heard its nickname: the caveman diet. That's cute. It gets at the heart of the idea—how the paleo diet is based on foods that our human ancestors would have eaten. But of course we can't really eat like a bunch of fur-clad nomads roaming the wilderness with spears, can we? The nickname only goes so far.

A better way to think about the paleo diet is to listen to your body. Pay attention to what happens when you chow down on a lot of processed grains. Notice the surge of energy when you bite into a hot, peppery steak. That's the paleo diet. It's the common sense that has been encoded into your DNA, thanks to those fur-clad nomads so many years ago. We don't need to act like cavemen, because we already carry their tastes and their hunger inside of us.

In many ways, our bodies are simple. They crave certain things—the kinds of things you find on the paleo diet. Listen to your body. You can be good as well as smart.

—The Editors at Sonoma Press

PART ONE

The Science Behind
the Paleo Diet

CHAPTER ONE

What Is the Paleo Diet?

The Paleolithic diet, caveman diet, or Paleo diet is a popular diet founded on the premise that our ancestors had a healthier diet and had better health than modern humans. Before the advent of agriculture, people were hunter-gatherers who subsisted on a diet of meats, fish, nuts, fruits, and vegetables rather than the refined sugars, dairy, grains, salt, and processed foods that are today's common foods.

The theory behind the Paleo diet is that the human body has not yet adapted to grain-based nourishment, which leads to many of the diseases plaguing contemporary society. Cardiovascular disease, obesity, diabetes, stroke, and even infertility can all be linked back to these modern diet changes because human beings are genetically hardwired to eat the hunter-gatherer diet that was followed for about 99.5 percent of human history. Studies have also shown that human brain function and physical ability peaked just before the agricultural revolution.

Why did our diet shift so dramatically? The simple answer is that human beings grouped together for support and companionship, which led to settling in one area rather than roaming around in search of food. This static lifestyle was conducive to agriculture and animal husbandry. Cereal grains and legumes became a convenient source of calories, and people stopped moving their bodies to forage and hunt for survival. This combination of inactivity and diet change has created an increasingly fat society that is actually malnourished due to a lack of nutrients in its food. Following the Paleo diet can address this nutrient deficit, and can be a huge step toward feeling and looking better.

What Do You Eat on the Paleo Diet?

We do not know definitively what our Paleo forebearers ate on a daily basis, and many foods they did consume are no longer available today because of evolution and extinction. The idea of the Paleo diet is to mimic the perceived caveman diet using modern food equivalents, refraining from anything that a caveman would not have been able to find. This means eliminating all processed foods, grains, legumes, processed sugars, processed oils, and dairy because these items came about after the agricultural and industrial revolutions. Since these "forbidden foods" make up the bulk of the standard American diet (SAD), many people are left wondering what exactly is on the Paleo menu.

Paleo-friendly foods include meats, fish, seafood, eggs, vegetables, fruit, healthy fats, nuts, tubers, and seeds. If you choose to follow a Paleo diet, you will be eating the freshest, healthiest, most nutrient-packed foods you can find, and cooking them in ways that do not add fats and calories to the finished dishes. These choices mirror what every medical professional and nutritionist has been recommending for years to produce vibrant, good health.

CHAPTER TWO

Gluten

The Danger in Plain Sight

I t is hard to believe that the slices of warm, crusty bread waiting in the bread basket can make you sick because they contain grain. If you think about all the foods you eat during a usual day and which ones contain some sort of cereal grain, you might feel as if you are in the middle of a diet minefield. Grains contain gluten, which can be dangerous to a surprising number of people.

Gluten is a sticky protein that is found in all the grains that are so prevalent in the modern diet. It can be very hard to digest and can irritate the body. Gluten is also what gives bread and baked products their lovely texture and structure, so many people do not want to stop eating it even if they have a gluten sensitivity. Gluten sensitivity is widely misunderstood and more far-reaching than many people realize. It is an autoimmune disease that creates chronic inflammation in all the organ systems in the body. This inflammation can occur if your digestive system is constantly weakened by gluten sensitivity so that it does not eliminate undigested proteins. The undigested proteins then float through the bloodstream instead, which creates an autoimmune reaction (Cordain, 2005).

One theory that addresses why gluten affects people negatively is that people have not adapted genetically to the gluten in wheat because cereal crops are a relatively new development in human evolution (Cordain, 2010). This theory is one of the foundations of the Paleo diet. People thrive and have fewer health issues if they follow a diet that restricts cereal grains as well as legumes, sugar, processed foods, refined oils, and dairy. Another reason there might be a very high prevalence of gluten sensitivity is that most of the cereal crops in the United States and other developed countries have been genetically enhanced to have a significantly higher gluten content. These types of crops have spread through natural means to infect almost all the crops regardless of the original strain. This means many (if not all) of the products made using cereal grains have levels of gluten that are not necessarily found in nature and are unfamiliar in the human diet (Fallon, 2011). Following a Paleo diet will help establish whether you are sensitive to gluten because symptoms you might not have attributed to gluten will lessen or vanish entirely. Some of the more easily recognizable symptoms of celiac disease and gluten sensitivity are:

- Gas or bloating
- Chronic constipation or diarrhea
- Pain or distension in the abdomen
- Unexplained weight loss
- A diagnosis of autoimmune diseases like lupus, asthma, or rheumatoid arthritis

- Unexplained joint or muscle pain
- Fatigue
- Depression or anxiety
- Anemia
- Infertility

Beyond the discomfort and negative impact on your health, it is important to get a definitive diagnosis of whether you have gluten issues, because if untreated this sensitivity can lead to an increased risk of premature death from diseases like cancer and heart disease. A study that covered 30,000 patients over 40 years showed a substantially increased risk of mortality, ranging from 35 percent for those who were gluten sensitive to a staggering 72 percent for those with gluten-related gut inflammation (Jönsson et al., 2005).

You actually might not know you are sensitive to gluten or have celiac disease because these issues can masquerade as other conditions. As many as 99 percent of people with gluten issues are undiagnosed but suffer from other health ailments, and do not realize that those ailments are caused by eating gluten. Gluten sensitivity is not just a minor inconvenience that means you have to avoid your favorite sandwich; *The New England Journal of Medicine* has pinpointed 55 diseases and conditions that can be caused or made worse by eating gluten (Farrell and Kelley, 2002). These diseases and conditions include:

- Depression
- Schizophrenia
- Inflammatory bowel disease
- Epilepsy
- Migraines
- Neuropathy
- Anxiety
- Addison's disease

- Autoimmune liver disease
- Dementia
- Autism
- Osteoporosis
- Irritable bowel disease
- Anemia
- Cancer
- Fatigue

- Canker sores
- Lupus
- Multiple sclerosis
- Thyroid disease

- Rheumatoid arthritis
- Sjorgren's disease
- Type 1 diabetes
- Epilepsy

The good news is that gluten sensitivity and celiac disease can be completely controlled with diet by eliminating sources of gluten. Many of these other conditions lessen or are cured when gluten is removed from the equation. While not all people suffering from these health concerns will have gluten sensitivity, it is prudent to rule that possibility out in order to discover the cause. Following the Paleo diet is one of the best strategies for identifying gluten sensitivity and helping eliminate many of the other chronic lifestyle-related diseases found in modern society.

How Does the Paleo Diet Address Diseases of Affluence?

The statistics are quite scary with respect to the health risks prevalent today. Starting a Paleo diet is a step in the right direction because it excludes many of the factors that contribute to these health issues. Many countries that are not rich have been showing an increase in these diseases, which begs the question of what might be the trigger point. Many scientists feel that a cereal-based diet could be the cause because people simply aren't physically equipped to handle it. This would explain at least some of the health reports showing a rise in cardiovascular disease and stroke in areas that are not urbanized or full of Western risk factors such as processed foods and a sedentary lifestyle. The mitigating factor could well be systematic inflammation and autoimmune reaction brought on by gluten sensitivity (Jönsson et al., 2005).

Studies that support this reasoning show that agrarian societies that initially started an agriculture-based diet about 500 generations ago have a lower occurrence of celiac disease than populations that shifted to a cereal-based diet between 1 and 100 generations ago. This might indicate that a genetic adaptation to this type of food has occurred over the generations. Certain foods can create a body-wide autoimmune reaction in a poorly adapted system, which can lead to many of the diseases of affluence (Jönsson et al., 2005). The Paleo diet eliminates both unhealthy grain-based carbohydrates and legumes, which are two of the foods that can cause this reaction.

Many popular diets insist that carbohydrates are very good for you, but this is not necessarily the case. Carbohydrates in the form of grains, sugar, and starchy vegetables can harm the mucous membranes in the digestive system. This makes it possible for harmful substances to enter the bloodstream, which can cause the immune system to produce antibodies against them. If this immune response becomes chronic, it can cause disease. High-carb diets have also been found to contribute to a heightened risk of cancer (Ryan, 2011). Cancer cells feed on sugar, so it is a good idea to starve them through a planned Paleo diet. Another consideration when eating carbohydrates is the impact this type of food has on blood sugar levels. Unstable spiking blood sugar created by eating high-glycemic foods can eventually lead to insulin resistance, diabetes, and even the development of metabolic disease.

Legumes are often used as a substitute for meat in vegetarian and vegan diets because they contain a great deal of protein. Unfortunately, most people do not know that legumes are also high in phytates (antioxidant compounds that can impair the absorption of nutrients), lectin (proteins that are inflammatory or toxic), and protease inhibitors (which inhibit the action of certain enzymes) (*Lectins in Dry Legumes,* 2011). It should be no surprise when considering its components that some legumes are actually poisonous if consumed raw. The lectins found in legumes are thought to be one of the causes of several diseases of affluence such as lupus and rheumatoid arthritis. The protease inhibitors in legumes hamper the process that breaks proteins into amino acids. All this means that eating legumes can create gastrointestinal issues or an autoimmune reaction, and can cause a protein and nutrient deficiency. Avoiding these types of foods by eating a Paleo diet seems to be a good strategy for continued good health and a decreased risk of many diseases.

Making Your Move to Paleo

CHAPTER FOUR

The Paleo Pantry

Transforming Your Kitchen and Food-Buying Habits

W hen you start your Paleo journey, it is imperative to clean out your pantry. Take a bag or box and empty out everything *not* recommended on the diet. Even if you are completely, irrevocably committed to the Paleo lifestyle, there will be moments of weakness when that box of Oreos looks pretty good. So why tempt yourself? Take your box of non-Paleo food to a local shelter or give it away to non-Paleo family and friends. Obviously, this pantry purging might not be possible if others in your home are not Paleo, but at least clear a section for yourself and add Paleo-friendly items. Some dry pantry items that are convenient to have on hand when preparing Paleo foods are:

- Your favorite spices and herbs

- Sea salt and cracked black pepper

- Nuts and seeds (almonds, sesame seeds, pistachios, sunflower seeds, pumpkin seeds, cashews, macadamia nuts, pecans, hazelnuts, and Brazil nuts)

- Dried fruit (raisins, cranberries, apricots, and blueberries)

- Cocoa powder

- Olives

- Sun-dried tomatoes

- Unsweetened applesauce

- Coconut and almond milk

- Nut butters

- Raw organic honey

- Gluten-free mustard

- Nama shoyu

- Dark chocolate

- Molasses

- Coconut oil

- Sesame oil

- Rice vinegar

- Apple cider vinegar

- Extra-virgin olive oil

- Almond and coconut flour

- Unsweetened shredded coconut

- Maple syrup

- Tahini

- Tomato paste

- Organic beef and chicken broth

- Hot sauce

- Coconut water

- Pumpkin (canned)

- Curry paste

- Canned tomatoes (no ingredients added)

- Organic tomato sauce

- Balsamic vinegar

- Pure vanilla extract

You also need to do a Paleo sweep through the fridge and freezer to remove any items not found in the diet. Replace these items with all the vegetables and fruits you want, lean meats and fish, and organic eggs.

You'll be amazed at the number of Paleo products available at your local market. Included are such items as Paleo tortillas, bread, crackers, nut butters, coconut oil, and coconut milk. Most markets now have online directories to their Paleo foods.

Good Paleo Diet Buying Habits

One of the biggest shocks to new Paleo enthusiasts is the cost of the food on the plan. This can often scare people away from continuing or even trying to eat Paleo in the first place. Fresh, healthy, whole foods are more expensive than processed convenience foods. But you don't need to bankrupt yourself to follow a Paleo diet plan. You just need to plan ahead, change the way you buy, and source out your food. You might also have to compromise on some of your choices in order to stay within your food budget. For example, if you want red grapes in the winter but they cost $10 per pound, you might have to rethink your choice and buy in-season tangerines instead.

Should You Buy Only Organic?

There is a great deal of research about organic versus conventionally farmed produce, and from a nutritional standpoint there is not much difference. However, there are some fruits and vegetables that are best purchased organic whenever your budget allows because they are considered to be the most contaminated by pesticides, herbicides, and other harmful agents. Since many of these foods figure prominently in Paleo recipes, it is best not to expose yourself to high levels of pollutants. The list includes apples, strawberries, peaches, hot peppers, nectarines, cucumbers, grapes, celery, cherry tomatoes, lettuce, spinach, bell peppers, kale, and zucchini.

The bottom line of the organic debate is try to buy produce that is fresh, local, and seasonal whenever possible. Shop at farmers' markets to get the best quality for the least amount of money. If you cannot find quality produce, it is always an option to get flash-frozen organic products in the frozen section of your local grocery store. You might lose a little of the nutritional value, but you can be sure about where the produce is from and what its designation is (organic or conventional). You'll also gain a bit of convenience for making smoothies, pastas, and casseroles.

Buying Paleo-Friendly Proteins

Protein is very important to the Paleo diet, so make sure you know how to get the best choices. Many basic Paleo guides and resources recommend eating only grass-fed or pasture-raised animals or birds and being aware of ecological concerns such as mercury contamination in fresh fish and seafood. You should take this into account when transforming your kitchen into a Paleo-friendly space. Learn to look at labels to determine where the protein is from, and be flexible enough to change your shopping list if a fabulous product comes up that is grass-fed or pasture-raised. Also, stock up when you see a Paleo staple on sale and freeze the extra portions.

If you truly cannot find the quality of protein you want to eat, look at frozen products for farm-raised options. There are many reputable companies freezing their meats and fish to reach consumers who do not have the luxury of fresh products. If you have to buy conventionally raised meats, look for lean cuts and trim any visible fat, because harmful elements such as antibiotics, hormones, and other toxins "live" in the fat. This fat also includes the skin on chicken, turkey, and duck, so strip it off before cooking or eating it. Other acceptable choices are elk, venison, and buffalo (bison), which are often raised on smaller farms and have a natural diet for at least part of their lives. Quality is key for your protein choices.

Break Out of a Buying-and-Eating Rut

Most people really know how to cook only about ten dishes and tend to rotate those throughout the month, breaking up the culinary monotony with processed meals or eating outside the home. When you start your Paleo lifestyle, you might find yourself eating the same thing all the time because it is a familiar way to cook or it uses your usual ingredients. This can lead to food boredom, which will make sticking with the Paleo plan very difficult. Embrace change and the foundations of the plan, which rest on eating a broad range of fresh, nutrition-rich foods. Buy new types of vegetables and fruits, experiment with meats you have never tried, and cook with combinations of unusual spices. When you are out shopping and see an ingredient that looks interesting and won't break the bank, put it in your basket and try it. There are many exciting food choices on the Paleo diet, so write your grocery list and do your shopping with an adventurous mindset. Don't just fill your cart and kitchen with familiar fruits and packages of prepared salads.

One of the most common mistakes people make when transitioning to the Paleo diet is eating too much fruit. Fruit salads are easy to make and don't require newfangled kitchen equipment or special items like tahini or coconut milk. The problem with this kind of "food monogamy" is that you will get too much sugar, which will make your blood sugar spike and sabotage any weight loss goals. Obviously, fruit has its place in a Paleo diet, but in moderation rather than as the main component in every meal. When you are shopping, focus on buying fruit such as apples, blueberries, and grapes, which are lower in natural sugars.

Nuts and seeds can be another pitfall on the Paleo diet because they are present in many recipes, both in their natural state and in the form of milk, flours, and butters. These foods are certainly healthy and act as grain substitutes in dishes, but they are also very high in fat and calories. People who expect to lose weight on a Paleo eating plan but who eat handfuls of nuts or seeds might find their weight actually going up instead of down. You should certainly have these products on hand in your Paleo-friendly kitchen, but with nuts and seeds the key is moderation and planning. If you are enjoying a piece of Paleo bread made with almond flour, don't top it with almond butter and wash it down with a glass of almond milk.

Understanding What You Are Buying

If you have done your research, you will know that there are very few processed food items on the Paleo diet beyond maple syrup, olives, and curry paste. What this means in practical terms is if you don't recognize something on the nutrition label, then the item is probably processed. Don't buy it. One of the activities you should be doing while shopping for the Paleo diet is reading labels before adding an item to your shopping cart. Some of the items found on labels will make it easy to weed out grains, dairy sweeteners, and other taboo ingredients, but other ingredients are a little more vague. For example, "natural sweeteners" could mean pretty much anything, so steer clear. Other words often used on a label actually mean wheat or sugar, but don't say those exact words. Some commonly used names on labels could include:

Gluten and wheat:

- Any ingredient with the word "wheat" in it
- Artificial flavoring
- Bleached flour
- Bread crumbs
- Bulgur
- Caramel color
- Cereal extract
- Couscous
- Cracker meal
- Dextrin
- Durum
- Einkorn
- Emmer
- Farina
- Flavorings
- Hydrolyzed vegetable protein (HVP)
- Kamut®
- Malt
- Matzo
- Modified food starch
- Monosodium glutamate (MSG)
- Natural flavoring
- Pasta (there are some nonwheat versions)
- Seasonings
- Seitan
- Semolina
- Spelt
- Triticale
- Vegetable protein
- Vegetable starch

Sugar:

- Agave nectar
- Barley malt syrup
- Beet sugar
- Brown sugar
- Cane crystals
- Caramel
- Carob syrup
- Corn sweetener
- Corn syrup
- Crystalline fructose
- Date sugar
- Dehydrated cane juice

- Dextran
- Dextrin
- Dextrose
- Diastase
- Diastatic malt
- Disaccharide
- Ethyl maltol
- Evaporated cane juice
- Fructose
- Fruit juice concentrate
- Galactose
- Glucose
- Golden syrup
- High-fructose corn syrup
- Invert sugar
- Lactose
- Malt syrup
- Maltodextrin
- Maltose
- Mannitol
- Monosaccharide
- Polysaccharide
- Raw sugar
- Ribose
- Rice syrup
- Saccharose
- Sorbitol
- Sorghum or sorghum syrup
- Sucrose
- Treacle
- Turbinado sugar
- Xylose

Read the nutrition labels very closely and have a handy list of all the words that can show up for soy, corn, and dairy as well, so you are aware of what you are putting into your body. When you transform your kitchen and buying habits to Paleo, it is all about mindful, informed shopping and stocking.

Tools and Equipment for a Paleo Kitchen

Preparing and cooking food for a Paleo diet can easily be done in a standard kitchen, but there are some culinary tools and equipment that will make it a great deal easier. This diet does take a little planning to do it right, so why not have the items on hand? This way you'll be able to follow the broadest range of recipes with the least amount of effort and fuss. The following are great additions to a Paleo kitchen:

- Blender
- Cast-iron skillet
- Food processor
- Hand mixer
- Mandoline
- Measuring cups
- Meat grinder
- Potato masher

- Professional chef knives
- Set of nesting bowls
- Slow cooker
- Steamer
- Storage containers
- Various baking pans and casserole dishes (muffin, cookie)
- Zester and grater

CHAPTER FIVE

Maintaining Paleo Outside Your Home

At Work, at School, Eating Out

E ven if you are having great success creating healthy Paleo meals at home, eventually you will have to go out to eat. Be aware that some things in your outside-the-home routine may be different now that you are eating a Paleo diet. Stopping for your usual cappuccino and bagel with cream cheese will not be on the schedule anymore, nor will picking up a fast-food lunch from a convenient restaurant. You need to change the ways you do things so that maintaining Paleo outside your home becomes familiar and easy.

Paleo at Work

The most important strategy for staying Paleo outside the home is to be prepared and bring your own lunch and snacks with you to work. There are some very ingenious lunch bags and containers available now because people are toting their food everywhere. Paleo lunches can be intricate or as simple as a salad topped with some cooked chicken or tuna. One handy option is to bring leftovers from your healthy Paleo dinner along with a couple of tasty snacks to work. There are countless delicious lunch options that make it easy to stay Paleo at work. Don't stress that you will have to explain your new lifestyle to people either, because many people bring their own lunches or will not be overly curious about yours. If anything, people might be jealous of how delicious your healthy lunch looks compared to their boring peanut butter sandwiches.

If someone does ask you about your new eating plan or comments on your glowing skin, by all means tell them you have embarked on the Paleo diet. Otherwise, try not to ambush your coworkers with criticisms about what they are eating or evangelize about the dos and don'ts of Paleo. This could just create tension. You can be enthusiastic about eating and feeling healthier without being self-righteous about it.

Paleo at School

Following a Paleo eating plan at home with kids can be challenging, because kids are inundated every day with media showing sugary, fat-laden food wrapped in bright kid-friendly packaging. In your own home, they will pretty much eat whatever you choose to serve and have in the house as snacks. When they leave the house for school, they will be confronted with loads of food options that will not be Paleo. You simply cannot micromanage their food choices from a distance. And, of course, cutting them off from important social interactions like dinner at a friend's house or Halloween parties is not the solution.

It is unrealistic to make non-Paleo food into "forbidden fruit" by banning all contact with it. This is the fastest way to have your kids trading their Paleo-friendly snack for a chocolate bar. Making Paleo food choices attractive and delicious is the best route. Instill healthy, informed eating habits in your children so they know what choices to make for themselves when you are not around. Kids love to learn about where food comes from and what it does in the body, and they can have fun experimenting with cooking and food preparation. Encourage kids to make their own lunches while talking about the importance of really high-quality foods and what junk food does to the body. Help them start their own little vegetable garden, if possible, to illustrate the difference between how a warm, sun-ripened tomato tastes in contrast to a store-bought one. Help them learn to identify and avoid foods that make them feel unwell. And make sure they know that eating a treat in moderation, such as a couple ounces of good-quality dark chocolate, is okay.

Your strategy for dealing with school and other children-oriented social events will also depend on the specific child. If your child has allergies, then by all means take steps to ensure they remain healthy by teaching your child what is safe to eat and informing other parents and teachers of your child's restrictions. If your child does not have food issues, it might be good to let them eat cake and ice cream in moderation at birthday parties and school events. This strategy allows them to fit in socially. In some cases, it will also let them feel exactly how those food choices affect the body. Even people with sugar addictions feel a little ill after a huge slice of frosted cake! Make sure you feed your child before the event so they won't be tempted to overdo it.

Paleo When Eating Out

Many people committed to a healthy lifestyle get stressed eating in restaurants even when they are not trying to eat a specifically Paleo diet. It can be intimidating looking at a menu and trying to pick appropriate dishes. Most restaurants do not take issues like fat, calories, or sodium into account when creating their menus. It is all about flavor, cost, and effective time management. The only time healthier meals will be in the forefront is when the intent is to produce a particular kind of dish. The culinary world is getting more aware of and active in the various diet concerns prevalent today. You often see special heart-healthy, gluten-free, or vegetarian dishes on the menu.

When eating out there are a few strategies you can follow to ensure you don't veer too far off the Paleo path. The strategy you employ will depend on how comfortable you are asserting yourself.

- Try to be the one who picks the restaurant. This might seem like a minor issue, but some restaurants have more Paleo options than others. It is a good idea to do a little research ahead of time by looking at the restaurant menu online. This will give you an idea of the type of food and cooking styles available. The only cuisine that is truly difficult to fit in a Paleo plan is Chinese because of the sauces and cooking ingredients. Some cities even have Paleo restaurants.

- When you get to the restaurant, do not be afraid to be that person who has special needs. Restaurants are very accommodating and have firm policies in place to make sure you have a good experience and you get the food you want. Ask questions about the ingredients and cooking processes to make sure you know what you are getting. Swap out your starches for a plate covered in vegetables and ask for all the dressings or sauces on the side. Stay away from fried items whenever possible and ask for simple grilled items. One good strategy is to simply tell your server that you are gluten and dairy sensitive, because most professional kitchen staffs are aware of how to create dishes that accommodate those issues.

- Sometimes you will be able to find items on menus that are Paleo friendly without having to make special requests of the staff. Remember that your goal is 80/20 when it comes to Paleo unless you are super strict with the diet plan or are very sensitive to gluten. If you do not react badly to gluten or lactose, then getting a little butter on your vegetables and seasoning salt on your steak will not be a problem. Always be courteous to the restaurant staff and indicate that you appreciate any extra effort they are making. The most important strategy when eating out is to enjoy your meal and the company without stressing.

CHAPTER SIX

Meal Plans

The First 30 Days

T his chapter provides you with a 30-day meal plan to get you started on your Paleo journey. The meal choices are not set in stone but are just guidelines, so feel free to switch the meals around. If you have leftovers from a dinner, you can use them for lunch the next day or even for breakfast. Throw a couple of tasty snacks into your lunch bag as well to round out your nutritional needs for the day.

Day 1

Breakfast: Tender Almond Pancakes
Lunch: Cream of Mushroom Soup
Dinner: Baked Salmon with Roasted Beets and Greens
Dessert: Lime Cookies

Day 2

Breakfast: Paleo "Oatmeal"
Lunch: Chicken Fruit Salad with Tangy Mustard Dressing
Dinner: Savory Beef Stew
Dessert: Chocolate Snack Cake

Day 3

Breakfast: Crunchy Almond Granola
Lunch: Turkey Burgers with Plum Salsa
Dinner: Tomato Baked Halibut
Dessert: Apple Pie Cupcakes with Spiced Frosting

Day 4

Breakfast: Banana French Toast
Lunch: Green Bean Salad
Dinner: Lemon Chicken
Dessert: Coffee Streusel Cake

Day 5

Breakfast: Breakfast Stir Fry
Lunch: Chicken, Pistachio, and Fig Salad
Dinner: Sole Florentine
Dessert: Chocolate Fondue

Day 6

Breakfast: Italian Vegetable Omelet
Lunch: Flank Steak with Caramelized Onions
Dinner: Spicy Pasta Puttanesca with Meat Sauce
Dessert: Slow-Cooked Peach and Plum Confit

Day 7

Breakfast: Swiss Chard Chicken Omelet
Lunch: Pad Thai
Dinner: Lamb Tagine
Dessert: Vanilla Bean Cream with Peaches

Day 8

Breakfast: Mint-Infused Melon Fruit Salad
Lunch: Gingered Carrot Soup
Dinner: Chicken Meatloaf
Dessert: Rich Chocolate Banana Pie

Day 9

Breakfast: Orange Cranberry Scones
Lunch: Ratatouille
Dinner: Beef Chow Mein
Dessert: Coconut Sorbet

Day 10

Breakfast: Breakfast Pudding
Lunch: Chicken Fajitas
Dinner: Grilled Halibut with Pepper Salsa
Dessert: Creamy Cheesecake

Day 11

Breakfast: Egg White Scramble
Lunch: Citrus Poached Salmon
Dinner: Slow-Cooked Chicken Korma
Dessert: Coconut Snowballs

Day 12

Breakfast: Chocolate Chip Strawberry Muffins
Lunch: Stuffed Butternut Squash
Dinner: Chili Lime Shrimp
Dessert: Pecan Pie

Day 13

Breakfast: Creamy Baked Eggs
Lunch: Barbecued Chicken Fingers
Dinner: Home-Style Meatloaf
Dessert: Poached Pears

Day 14

Breakfast: Paleo Breakfast Sausage
Lunch: Texas Chili
Dinner: Osso Buco
Dessert: Mango Almond Custard

Day 15

Breakfast: Blueberry Crumble Muffins
Lunch: Gingered Lemon Broccoli Salad
Dinner: Chicken Shepherd's Pie
Dessert: Spiced Pear and Applesauce

Day 16

Breakfast: Sweet Potato Hash
Lunch: Chicken Vegetable Wraps
Dinner: Pork Chops with Spiced Apples and Thyme
Dessert: Decadent Chocolate Mousse

Day 17

Breakfast: Apple Paleo Muffins
Lunch: Sesame Turkey Meatballs
Dinner: Blackened Tilapia
Dessert: Cantaloupe Granita

Day 18

Breakfast: Zucchini, Asparagus, and Chicken Frittata
Lunch: African Sweet Potato Soup
Dinner: Venison with Mustard and Herbs
Dessert: Dark Chocolate Pots de Crème

Day 19

Breakfast: Spiced Banana Coconut Waffles
Lunch: Butternut Squash Soup
Dinner: Almond-Crusted Chicken
Dessert: Slow-Cooked Carrot Pudding

Day 20

Breakfast: Baked Eggs in Salsa
Lunch: Vegetable Chicken Stir Fry
Dinner: Roasted Salmon with Fennel
Dessert: Fresh Gingered Cantaloupe

Day 21

Breakfast: Orange French Toast
Lunch: Spicy Chicken Soup
Dinner: Beef Short Ribs
Dessert: Lemon Slices

Day 22

Breakfast: Eggs Florentine
Lunch: Curried Chicken "Couscous"
Dinner: Cajun Spiced Salmon
Dessert: Toffee Apples

Day 23

Breakfast: Vanilla Quinoa Cereal
Lunch: Lettuce Wraps with Spicy Chicken
Dinner: Beef Stroganoff
Dessert: Strawberry Ice Cream

Day 24

Breakfast: Roasted Red Pepper Sausage Omelet
Lunch: Tuscan Tomato Soup
Dinner: Pork and Apple Casserole
Dessert: Molten Chocolate Lava Cake

Day 25

Breakfast: Mediterranean Vegetable Frittata
Lunch: Shrimp and Peach Tostadas
Dinner: Chicken Cacciatore
Dessert: Vanilla Custard

Day 26

Breakfast: Banana Vanilla Pancakes
Lunch: Herbed Meatballs
Dinner: Scallops with Grilled Pineapple Salsa
Dessert: Chocolate Mug Cake

Day 27

Breakfast: Chocolate Raspberry Donuts
Lunch: Chicken Noodle Salad with Thai Dressing
Dinner: Grainy Mustard–Crusted Pork Tenderloin
Dessert: Apple Crumble

Day 28

Breakfast: Quinoa Porridge
Lunch: Stuffed Bell Peppers
Dinner: Moroccan Chicken
Dessert: Ambrosia with Coconut and Almonds

Day 29

Breakfast: Portobello Mushroom Eggs Florentine
Lunch: Broccoli Turkey Slaw
Dinner: Mediterranean Fish Stew
Dessert: Pineapple Gelato

Day 30

Breakfast: Sweet Potato Quiche
Lunch: Grilled Lamb Skewers
Dinner: Shrimp Paella
Dessert: Barbecued Peaches with Cinnamon

CHAPTER SEVEN

10 Steps for Success

Congratulations for making the decision to step on the path to a healthier lifestyle through the Paleo diet! You might be wondering exactly how to make the switch to the diet. As with most things in life, the most difficult part of getting started is actually starting. Here are 10 steps that will help you transition to the Paleo lifestyle and to succeed.

1. Accept Your Imperfections: Sometimes the reason people fail when trying new eating plans or lifestyle changes is because they have unrealistic expectations. They also put too much pressure on themselves to be perfect. Paleo should make you feel better, stronger, and healthier, so beating yourself up over any tiny slip in eating is not part of the strategy. Paleo is not a sprint, either; it is a lifestyle choice. The goal is to try to create a plan that is a minimum of 80 percent Paleo that you can stick to and enjoy. You should not feel deprived because you can't have one of your mother's famous rum balls or castigate yourself because you *did* have a rum ball. Do your best and live your life with joy, not as if you are in culinary prison.

2. Personalize the Paleo Diet: All Paleo enthusiasts are not created equal when it comes to what they eat and how much. Remember that learning about Paleo is just the start, and that you need to tailor this diet to your own life. The range of foods available in this eating plan is extensive, so your Paleo experience might be very different from your co-worker's, who has type 2 diabetes. For example, the Paleo groups that have been studied, such as the Inuit in the Arctic and the Tukisenta in New Guinea, had extremely divergent diets and both thrived (Gadsby, 2004). You need to find the template that works for you and your health goals. Everyone also starts at a different place, which means your Paleo diet will evolve as you follow it for 30 days, 6 months, 1 year, or 5 years. Your physical activity, genetics, general health, goals, and eating habits will all come into play when planning your Paleo strategy. You might have to experiment to see what works for you with regard to what foods to include and the quantity and frequency of meals.

3. Eat Enough Carbohydrates: Carbohydrates have gained an extremely negative reputation in most diet groups over the past few decades. People think carbohydrates are the chief contributors to weight gain and create spikes in blood sugar. This is true for some carbohydrates, but carbs are not created equal with respect to nutrition. Weight gain cannot be blamed exclusively on carbohydrate consumption because many other factors such as hormone imbalance and inactivity can play a role. Paleo does limit carbohydrates from grains, legumes, and sugar sources, but allows healthy carbs that are also high in fiber, such as green vegetables, berries, sweet potato, dried fruits, and squash. So make sure you eat enough of these Paleo-friendly carbohydrates to reduce food cravings and help you to avoid eating inappropriate choices.

4. Eat Enough Fat: Fat is another casualty in the diet wars along with carbohydrates, and many people ruthlessly cut out all forms of fat from their food. This is a mistake. Fat and carbohydrates are the primary sources used to fuel the body, so limiting them can make your energy level almost nonexistent. You will find yourself hungry all the time if you do not have enough fat in your diet. Also, fats are essential for the effective functioning of almost every part in the body, from the skin to the heart and all the internal organs. Eating the right kinds of fat can also help reduce inflammation in the body, which cuts the risk of many serious health conditions and diseases. The fats you should include in your diet are essential fats that the body needs to get from healthy food sources (omega-3 and omega-6 fatty acids), monounsaturated fats, saturated fats, and polyunsaturated fats. The fats you will avoid in Paleo are refined fats such as those found in processed vegetable oils.

5. Remember, Paleo Is Not Just Food: When you first start your Paleo journey it will literally be all about the food. What are you going to eat, the food you can't eat, and the items you will crave in the first few weeks. Diet and food choices are certainly the foundation of the Paleo lifestyle, but the end goal is to feel healthier, which means other factors are also important. You could be following a strict Paleo eating plan, but if you neglect exercise, sleep, and stress management, your diet will not be as effective. If you ignore these other aspects of the Paleo lifestyle, you probably will not reach your goals, which can negatively impact your commitment to Paleo.

Sleep in particular is absolutely crucial for good health, and it is usually the first thing we skimp on when our busy lives take over. The human body requires sleep for many important reasons, ranging from minor to deadly. Some of the effects of not enough sleep are:

- Hormones such as human growth hormone are not released

- Depression or grumpiness

- More accidents due to lack of focus

- Risk of serious diseases such as cardiovascular disease, diabetes, and stroke

- Loss of memory and concentration

- Impaired stress management

- Decreased athletic performance

- Lack of sex drive

- Weight gain

Along with sleep, you need to move. The foundation of the Paleo diet is eating in a manner that humans are meant to eat, and this idea also covers moving your body the way our ancestors moved. This does not mean hours in the gym but rather something that gets your blood pumping and muscles working. Exercise can be walking or playing with your dog, dancing, playing a sport, or even gardening. Exercise has many benefits, including lowering your risk of many diseases, improving the immune system, weight loss, helping you sleep better, and reducing stress. Stress can kill you, so it is important to learn to either reduce the stress in your life or manage it with exercise or meditation.

6. Commit Fully to the Lifestyle: Paleo is not for everyone, but it is important to commit to the Paleo diet for a minimum of 30 days to see if it is for you. The benefits of this diet will not be apparent if you only eat 50 percent Paleo, because you will never purge from your system all the toxins from years of gluten, sugar, and dairy consumption. How can you witness your reaction to these foods if you cheat and never detox? After the first strict 30-day cycle on Paleo, it is acceptable to drop to an 80 percent plan as long as your food choices do not produce a negative reaction in your body. You might be surprised to discover that your chronic digestion issues, fatigue, weight gain, and insomnia are caused by your food. Make the commitment so you can make an informed choice about whether you can continue to eat Paleo permanently.

7. Research the Diet: If you are considering the Paleo diet, there is a good chance you have read a few books and looked up specifics on the Internet. Getting all the information possible about what to expect, what foods to eat or not eat, and the science behind the diet is important. Paleo is not a simple, quick diet that is as easy as drinking a few shakes or eliminating a particular category of food. It requires planning and commitment to achieve your goals. Also, if you plan to start a Paleo lifestyle, take the time to review your budget and where you currently get your food, because you might need to make some changes. Quality food can be more expensive than junk, and sourcing grass-fed meats can be a lot of work. You should be ready to devote more time to both shopping and preparation of the food in order to succeed in the transition to Paleo. This can actually be a very positive experience, because creating a closer, more informed relationship with your food can make eating much more pleasurable. You will find yourself looking at Paleo cookbooks and experimenting with all sorts of techniques and ingredients that are adventuresome and new.

8. Don't Become Obsessed: It is easy to become consumed with all aspects of Paleo to your detriment. You should, of course, be a mindful eater and informed about this lifestyle choice, but try not to get lost in the details. One thing to avoid is fixating on the whole caveman theory of the Paleo diet. You really do not need to know all the scientific details in order to follow the plan. Knowing the basics behind the choices is good, but that is not what will motivate you to stay on plan when confronted by a warm donut. Almost everything we eat today is different from what early human beings ate, so don't get fanatical about organic wine or whether a kiwi grew in certain region. Simply avoid grains, refined sugars, refined oils, legumes, and dairy. And, if you do not recognize an ingredient, don't eat the food. You will be eating a majority of your foods in a relatively natural state. But if you are curious about a packaged item, read the label and look for a short list filled with recognizable items.

Do not be obsessed with calories on the Paleo diet. Many people who start a Paleo diet are hoping to lose weight, yes. Calories do count in Paleo to a certain extent, because if you consume more calories than you burn, you will gain weight. And you can't simply eat whatever you want on Paleo with no consideration of nutritional analysis. But it is hard to overeat on Paleo if you make sure to add lots of variety to your diet. Moderate your portions, and make sure the majority of your plate is filled with healthy starches, colorful produce, and lean protein bursting with nutrients. Do not make the mistake of eating too many fruits and nuts or making almond butter the foundation of every meal. Soon you will find that your body is regulating itself: You will have fewer cravings and will be less apt to overeat.

9. Know Why You Are Eating Paleo: The Paleo lifestyle requires you to be prepared in many different ways, including mentally, to tackle the various challenges. There definitely will be challenges to face with Paleo, from initial detox symptoms, food cravings, and social pressure, to slipping willpower. Preparing yourself mentally and understanding exactly why you want to embark on this diet plan is crucial to success. When confronted with a fresh-baked loaf of crusty bread, you need to be very clear in your own mind why you want to consciously make the choice to abstain. It is worth all the effort in the end. Do not visualize Paleo as the "can't have foods" but rather as the goal of vibrant good health. Learn to listen to your body so that you eat when hungry (not when bored or stressed), sleep when you are tired, and play when you need a break.

10. Surround Yourself with Support: People succeed at lifestyle changes when they have a buddy system or supportive family and friends to back them up. When you have weak moments or need a cheering section, this type of community can mean the world of difference. A support system also makes you accountable for your choices and reminds you of the important goals that precipitated your switch to Paleo. If you simply cannot find anyone in your immediate circle who is a good choice for this supporting role, then seek out a Paleo community online or locally that can provide answers and encouragement. There are countless enthusiastic people on blogs, on forums, and in networking groups, who are on the Paleo journey themselves and want to help you become a success story. You might find yourself in the gratifying position of providing the needed information and cheering on someone else as well.

Building Your Own Paleo Diet

13. Has your weight changed in the past six months? If so, how?

14. Has your health changed in the past six months?

Eating Habits

15. Do you eat breakfast?

16. How many caffeinated beverages do you drink per day?

17. How much sugar do you eat per day?

18. Do you eat a lot of grains and legumes?

19. How much meat do you eat per day?

20. Do you have one or more alcoholic beverages a day?

21. How many servings of vegetables and fruits do you eat per day?

22. Do you eat three large meals, or do you graze throughout the day?

23. Can you tell when you are full?

24. What kind of snacks do you eat?

25. Do you eat a variety of foods each day or do you stick with favorites?

The Paleo diet takes planning and organizing, because you must source out and prepare a variety of high-end organic products. If you live in a remote area with no shopping options or you are time-starved, it can be very difficult to prepare healthy foods. You will need to commit to more time in the kitchen or think outside the box for solutions.

Reading labels and understanding why foods are healthy or damaging is crucial for Paleo enthusiasts, so take some time to research this eating plan thoroughly before jumping into it. You will also need to commit to the other aspects of a Paleo lifestyle, such as exercise, good sleep, and a positive mental state. Knowing the answers to the listed lifestyle questions will arm you to meet some of the challenges of starting on the diet. You should always consult a medical professional before embarking on a drastic life transformation, especially if your weight or health has changed over the past six months.

The preceding eating habits questions will give you a good idea about where you are starting from and what the detox experience might entail for you. If you eat a great deal of sugar, grains, and caffeine, for example, you may find that you will have more severe symptoms of withdrawal from these products. Your body will essentially clean itself out of all the accumulated toxins from unhealthy food choices, and if your diet was very unhealthy, this purge might last longer (*Protein: Moving Closer to Center Stage,* 2009). Some of the detox symptoms you might experience when starting Paleo include:

- Headaches or mental fogginess

- Food cravings

- Fatigue and dizziness

- Irritability or mood swings

- Digestion issues such as constipation, nausea, or diarrhea

- Body aches

- Increased urination

- Increased thirst and appetite

The best strategy to ensure success on Paleo is to be honest about where you are starting from, in answering the lifestyle and eating-habit questions, because that will tell you how to proceed.

Q & A

CHAPTER NINE

The Paleo Diet for Special Dietary Needs

Paleo is a healthy diet choice if done with planning and education, but it can be ineffective if you simply cut out everything on the restricted list and do not consume a variety of foods. It can actually be damaging if you do not get all the nutrients required for optimal health. Anyone embarking on a lifestyle change such as the Paleo diet should consult a health provider to ensure that there are no negative considerations—especially if you have any existing health condition or specific special dietary needs. Your Paleo choices will need to be particularly well thought out, to make sure you address your needs. People with special dietary needs could include those with the following conditions, as well as children.

Pregnant and Nursing Women

Anyone who is pregnant will be aware of the necessity of a healthy diet high in iron, folate, and essential fatty acids, and the Paleo diet delivers these nutrients. Iron is crucial because it performs many tasks in the body, such as carrying oxygen in the blood, supporting enzyme function, and helping the muscles use and store oxygen. Iron deficiency can create issues in the mother but it can also cause a higher risk of premature birth. Folate is also crucial for both the growing baby and the mother. Folate assists with the maintenance and healthy growth of new cells, and a deficiency can cause low birth weight and premature birth along with slower development (*Prenatal Nutrition,* 2011). Essential fatty acids are often included in prenatal vitamins because they support fetal brain development and can help reduce the risk of postpartum depression.

If you are pregnant and eating on the Paleo plan, you must include plenty of organ meats, salmon, spinach, red meat, asparagus, dark leafy green vegetables, broccoli, walnuts, avocado, oysters, and clams in your meals to ensure a good supply of these nutrients. Keep in mind, though, that you will probably have to modify your Paleo diet slightly to accommodate your pregnancy, because most pregnant women do not tolerate a high-protein diet. So listen to your body and reduce the protein amount a bit while increasing healthy carbohydrates and foods containing essential fatty acids.

Vegetarians and Vegans

It might surprise you to realize that Paleo is often the last stop on the diet journey for many vegans and vegetarians. It seems like a strange culinary jump to go from no meat to a meat-inclusive diet, but the leap is actually not that far. Most vegetarians and vegans are extremely health conscious and nutritionally informed people who understand the foundations of the Paleo diet. The Paleo diet, when followed as it is meant to be, eliminates eating meat from animals that have been raised in commercial and factory environments. This difference is often enough to alleviate the guilt and satisfy the social consciousness that motivates many vegetarians.

Other vegans and vegetarians may be simply looking for a diet that will make them feel great and help them get healthier. Paleo fits those needs and does not include some of the nutritional deficiencies associated with vegetarianism, like insufficient iron and vitamin B12. If you want to eat Paleo because it makes sense to you but you also want to remain a vegetarian, there are some obstacles. The Paleo diet does not encourage eating some of the main protein sources vegetarians eat, such as grains and soy. What is there left to eat for protein as a Paleo vegetarian? Vegetables, fruit, nuts, eggs, and seeds, plus some dairy and tofu to comprise your 20 percent non-Paleo foods so you get sufficient protein. You should definitely take a vitamin B12 supplement to avoid serious health issues. It is difficult to maintain good health eating this diet without the meat, so be very careful and monitor your body closely.

Type 2 Diabetes

Diabetes fits into the category of diseases that are caused by poor diet and lifestyle choices such as lack of exercise. The modern diet, full of sugar and carbohydrates, is damaging to the process in the body that regulates blood sugar, creating issues like insulin resistance and obesity, which in turn contribute to type 2 diabetes. Diabetes has become an epidemic in our society, and diet is a key treatment choice for many people.

Paleo may not be the first choice for some people with diabetes, but it is a very healthy option, because protein, healthy low-glycemic carbs, and fats do not cause damaging spikes in blood sugar. Wholesome unprocessed organic foods without toxins, refined sugar, dairy, or gluten do not cause inflammation and an auto-immune response in the body, which is also linked to diabetes. If you have diabetes, you should limit your fruit intake, particularly dried fruits, because they are higher in natural sugar. You should also limit your carbohydrate choices, while consulting the glycemic index, when planning your Paleo meals to ensure that you control what you eat.

Metabolic Syndrome

Metabolic syndrome is not a disease but rather a cluster of risk factors that, when combined, create an increased risk of heart attack, stroke, and diabetes. The cluster includes high cholesterol, high blood sugar, abdominal fat, and high blood pressure. Metabolic syndrome is thought to affect one in six people in the United States (Staff, 2013). The good news is this syndrome can be controlled and even eliminated by good diet choices and increased exercise. The diet guidelines put forth for treatment of metabolic syndrome resemble the basic Paleo diet quite closely. If you have this syndrome, you can tweak the Paleo diet to create the biggest positive impacts quite easily.

Some of the changes include limiting carbohydrate consumption (fruits and starchy tubers) and steering clear of too much palmitic and myristic saturated fat found in grain-fed animals. If you have metabolic syndrome, your best strategy is to follow the Paleo diet strictly rather than cheating frequently. Concentrate on wholesome, completely unprocessed food, and highlight lean meats and vegetables. Also, make sure you are exercising regularly, sleeping enough, and handling your stress to ensure your diet efforts won't be sabotaged by other lifestyle factors.

Autoimmune Disorders and Digestive Problems

Issues that are systemwide or concentrated in your digestive system can be very debilitating, and they may require special dietary attention to control or cure the condition. Some of the most common issues that fall into these categories are Crohn's disease, lupus, celiac disease, irritable bowel syndrome, multiple sclerosis, and rheumatoid arthritis. Eating a Paleo diet is a good start, but you have to accept that improvements might take time to manifest. So give the diet a chance before giving up.

There are some strict diet rules when dealing with these types of issues that are quite similar to Paleo, such as eliminating legumes, sugar, grains, dairy, and vegetable oils. Other limitations to consider are removing anything containing yeast, nuts and seeds, nightshade vegetables (tomatoes, eggplant, potatoes, and all peppers), and egg whites. You should also cut down on fruit consumption, because sugar can exacerbate some of these conditions. Make sure you also closely follow the Paleo recommendations concerning exercise, sleep, and stress.

Chronic Kidney Disease

About one in nine adults in the United States has chronic kidney disease, and the percentage is rising because other serious conditions such as diabetes and high blood pressure put a great deal of stress on the kidneys. One positive aspect of this issue is that if you stop creating a negative environment in the body for the kidneys, you can reverse or control kidney disease. The Paleo diet can be a good choice for people with kidney disease, because it eliminates many of the foods that contribute to the condition, such as sugar and processed foods.

Be very careful when eating Paleo with a kidney condition, because some aspects of Paleo can make things worse. The most important consideration is that too much protein can be an issue for people with chronic kidney disease. High-protein diets can accelerate kidney function loss (*About Chronic Kidney Disease,* 2013). People who have chronic kidney disease should also limit phosphorus, sodium, and potassium. This means limiting meats, nuts, chocolate, seeds, some fruits and vegetables, and starchy vegetables. Research your foods to make sure you aren't overindulging in foods that are high in these nutrients.

Cancer

The word *cancer* can strike terror into the heart of most people, because cancer is so prevalent and so many things seem to contribute to the risk of getting this disease. Many cancers are preventable or treatable with diet adjustments, and the Paleo diet is a good choice for some people who have certain cancers. One aspect of Paleo that seems to support a positive impact on cancer is that it eliminates sugar. Recent cancer studies have shown that cancer cells break down glucose 200 times faster than healthy cells and have about 16 times more insulin receptors. This is called the Walburg effect, and means a diet that does not provide this sugary fuel source (like Paleo) actually starves the cancer cells (Heiden and Thompson, 2011). Low-carbohydrate diets and insulin potentiation therapy are becoming quite common as cancer treatment options. There are no studies that track the effect of a Paleo diet on cancer, but the diet does conform very closely to the diet recommended by the American Cancer Society. Paleo also contributes to general good health through exercise, sustainable weight loss, sleep, and stress management, which is beneficial for any person fighting cancer.

Children

Paleo can be extremely beneficial for growing kids, but there are some considerations when introducing children to the diet. From a health standpoint, wholesome, nutritious foods are infinitely better than the standard fat and sugar-laden kid-targeted foods. The trick is to get kids to understand that it is a fun and interesting diet, not just a set of restrictions. Keep in mind that children with growing brains need more healthy carbohydrates than adults do, so make sure your kids gets plenty of sweet potatoes and other starchy fruits or vegetables. Take it meal by meal, lead by example, and have patience.

CHAPTER TEN

The Paleo Diet for Athletes

F or many athletes, carbohydrates are the foundation of their diets, and the idea of replacing carbs with healthy fat and protein can cause horror. However, there are enough studies and testimonials from world-class athletes that suggest that a Paleo diet can not only optimize performance but can also prolong professional careers. It just takes a bit of faith to try it.

What About Paleo and Athletic Performance?

Professional athletes are undeniably fit, but are they healthy? Physical fitness and health often do not go hand in hand, because some athletes push themselves hard enough to cause damage from overtraining and do not allow enough time for the body to recover. The nutritional needs of athletes change, depending on what stage of their training they are in and how far they push themselves. Most athletes' bodies are in a constant state of recovery, which is dependent on getting adequate rest and making good diet choices. Athletes should maintain a consistent protein level, which is a little lower than a basic Paleo plan. As the training intervals increase in intensity, so should healthy carbohydrate consumption in order to ensure that the demands of the body are met. When training intervals drop off during periods for resting the body, it is important to cut calories to maintain a healthy weight.

One myth that is still prevalent in the athletic world is that carbohydrates or glucose is the best form of fuel for endurance (Kravitz, 2013). Anyone who has hit the dreaded wall in marathon running can tell you that running out of glucose as fuel can be catastrophic. In many cases you simply cannot pack your body with enough glucose to maintain peak performance. By adapting your body to burn fat instead, you ensure that you have more than enough fuel for your physical needs. Even an athlete with 6 percent body fat has about 30,000 fat calories to draw from, which is like having a full tank of gas and only using half of it in a race. Most athletes would love that resource.

One of the effects of being a serious athlete, whether professional or just a dedicated amateur, is that pushing yourself physically can lead to premature aging, which can end careers. When the body is pushed physically to its limits and it is only taking in low carbohydrates, it will produce fuel bodies created from fat called ketones, which can fight oxidative stress. Intense training can produce chronic oxidative stress, which will age you if you don't combat it with something like the Paleo diet (Sohal and Weindruch, 1996). The Paleo diet can also lower the acid levels in the body, which can promote protein synthesis in the muscles and also reduce the effects of aging.

Are There Any Changes to Paleo for Athletes?

An athlete's typical Paleo diet day could include chicken breasts, almonds, coconut oil, avocados, dark leafy greens, eggs, lean beef, onions, and nonsoy- or nondairy-based protein powder. This would mean that your calories would be broken down to approximately 30 percent from protein, 30 percent from fats, and 40 percent from healthy carbohydrates. This is very different from the standard diet athletes follow, which is about 60 percent from carbohydrates, 20 percent from protein, and 20 percent from fats. The Paleo diet should be coupled with low-repetition, heavyweight resistance training along with interval training. This Paleo approach is meant to force the body to burn fat as fuel, add strength and muscle without gaining weight, and keep natural testosterone levels high.

To achieve peak performance and maintain optimal health, some athletes might have to modify the standard Paleo diet a little. An athlete puts much greater stress on the body than the most active Paleo ancestor would have experienced. Sustained 15 to 35 hours a week of intense training creates precisely targeted nutrition needs. Because the Paleo diet is comparatively lower in carbs, it is thought to be extremely well suited to sports such as gymnastics and diving, but can be difficult for endurance athletes to follow without some changes. Some of the adjustments that athletes should make to the basic Paleo plan could include the following:

- Eat a 600-calorie meal that is low fiber, low protein, low fat, and low on the glycemic index about two hours before starting a workout or race.

- If you are participating in a short training or event, under an hour, hydrate during the physical activity with water only. If your workout or race is over an hour, try to have a liquid boost that contains ingredients high on the glycemic index. If you don't have time to make your own beverage, use a sports drink that is not full of additives and unpronounceable ingredients.

- There may be points in particularly intense training intervals when it might be necessary to consume a higher percentage of starchy veggies, and even some legumes or grains, to get enough calories and nutrients. Just make sure your choices are whole, unprocessed foods.

- After your training or race, consume a drink that contains about five times more carbohydrates than protein, and drink it within 30 minutes of finishing so that you can recover effectively.

- If you are not eating dairy products, make sure you get enough calcium through your food sources to avoid the risk of a stress fracture due to a deficiency. Include almond milk, spinach, salmon, or sardines in your diet or take a 1,200- to 1,500-mg supplement.

- At least for three to four hours after your race, continue to consume foods or drinks that are about 80 percent carbohydrate and 20 percent protein. This time frame is where you might want to load up on your non-Paleo food allotment, such as pasta and rice, or stick to Paleo foods like sweet potatoes or dried fruit. Your goal is foods high on the glycemic index.

CHAPTER ELEVEN

The Paleo Diet for Weight Loss

One of the most common reasons people consider the Paleo diet is that they want to shed excess pounds. It is just another diet in a long line of options tried and discarded rather than a lifestyle choice that has weight loss as a side effect rather than a goal. Will you lose weight when eating Paleo? Maybe. Just because you are eating wholesome, good-quality food does not mean you can eat mindlessly. Weight loss is certainly possible with Paleo, but the goal should be good health (lower cholesterol, blood pressure, and blood sugar) rather than a drop in the numbers on your scale. If weight loss is your goal, then you should be aware of what food does in the body and how to increase the probability of success.

How Is Weight Determined in the Body?

Weight loss can certainly occur when eating the Paleo diet. Depending on your starting diet and physical shape, the weight loss might be very dramatic. The Paleo diet cuts out some of the biggest contributors to weight gain, such as processed foods, refined sugar, carbohydrates, and sodium. Some of that early weight loss will be water rather than fat, but it will be motivating regardless of composition. That type of weight loss will not be sustainable, though, so don't be discouraged when your scale starts posting a more realistic two-pounds-a-week loss.

Long-term weight loss on Paleo will depend entirely on your approach to the diet and commitment to healthy eating in general. If you follow the general guidelines for Paleo eating, you should not be hungry when trying to lose weight or maintaining your current numbers. Protein and fiber-packed vegetables are filling, which eliminates the need to snack or fill up with empty calorie choices. Simply eat when you are hungry and stop when you are full. You can still enjoy delicious gluten-free desserts and tasty snacks when eating Paleo, so don't think of all the food items you will be missing but rather the delicious options available every day.

Eating a healthy, nutrient-packed diet is often a new idea for people who are used to restricting calories, fat, and carbohydrates in a vicious diet cycle. It can be scary to eat real portions and feel full. Restricting calories is the first strategy for most people when they diet, and they often don't realize that simple subtraction does not mean weight loss. After an initial drop in weight, the body adapts to calorie deprivation by cutting the amount of energy expended, lowering the metabolism. Prolonged calorie restriction can create a permanent low metabolism, making weight loss almost impossible. You need to eat to maintain a healthy weight *and* to lose pounds. Nutritious foods eaten when hungry combined with other healthy lifestyle choices like exercise are a better long-term recipe for weight loss than deprivation.

If you find that you are not losing weight when eating a Paleo diet, there are some possible reasons. Most of the issues preventing a healthy weight loss can be adjusted quite easily with some planning and modification. Read on, to learn the most common causes.

Stress

Stress can create many issues in the body, with weight gain or stalled weight loss right at the top of the list (Maglione-Garves, 2005). When we are stressed, the body releases a steroid hormone called cortisol that assists in the "fight or flight" survival response. This is a good thing from an evolutionary standpoint, but in today's high-stress environment, people often do not get a chance to turn off this process, which leads to too much cortisol in the blood. This in turn can lead to a slew of damaging physical issues such as blood sugar imbalance, decrease in muscle tissue, and increased fat in the abdominal area. Managing your stress is crucial for weight loss and health in general.

Genetics

It is a fact that everyone's body looks different. And sometimes the body is a certain weight because that is where it operates at optimum levels. Most people with jobs and commitments other than creating the perfect six-pack abs will not look like underwear models. This is not to say that you can't look like a model, but rather that it might be unrealistic and unhealthy to do so. Women naturally need more fat than men for fertility and health reasons, and dropping too far on the scale can be detrimental to your health. Instead of stressing about a number on the scale and perhaps having unrealistic expectations about what you should look like, think about how you feel. Do you have energy and fewer physical issues? This is more important.

You Don't Realize You *Are* Losing Weight

If you are simply jumping on your bathroom scale and looking at a number, you might not be getting the entire weight-loss picture. If you have added exercise and Paleo eating to your routine, there is a good chance you are adding muscle to your frame and increasing bone density. These changes add weight because muscle weighs more than fat. You could hypothetically drop 10 pounds of fat and not know it by the scale. The best way to tell if you have changed the composition of your body is a body fat percentage test. But looking at how your clothes fit, as well as at the lines of your body, can also show you your progress.

Not Enough Exercise

Paleo is not just about the food; it also recommends moving your body. Sustained low-impact daily exercise will help burn fat. You don't need to head for the gym for marathon sessions of heart-pounding exercise to lose weight. Exercise can mean walking briskly, dancing, playing a sport, gardening, or even playing with your dog. You can certainly participate in a more vigorous routine, but it isn't necessary. Weight training should eventually become part of your fitness regimen because muscle burns more calories than fat, and lifting weights can reduce your risk of osteoporosis later in life. So if your weight loss has stalled, ramp up your physical activity or change the kind of exercise you are doing.

Eating Too Much

Paleo is not magic. If you eat too much, you will gain weight even if the food is organic grass-fed beef raised by hand. Calories do matter, so if you find your weight stalling at a certain point, look closely at what you are eating. Starting a food journal at the beginning of the Paleo journey is also a great idea, because it makes you accountable for what you put in your mouth. It also helps you to course-correct if needed. Some people who do an 80 percent Paleo plan pick really bad foods for the other 20 percent, such as cheesecake or junk food. Keep all your choices healthy and be realistic about portion sizes so you do reach your weight goal.

Not Enough Sleep

Sleep deprivation causes the release of cortisol the same way stress can, and studies have shown that people who do not sleep enough gain weight (Hu, 2008). There are two hormones that are crucial in the weight loss process. They are ghrelin, which tells you when to eat, and leptin, which tells you to stop eating. Persons who are sleep deprived have more ghrelin, less leptin, and a slower metabolism, which is a nonproductive combination with respect to body weight. Also when you are chronically tired, you will be more apt to reach for a quick energy boost containing sugar and less apt to exercise. You must get seven to eight hours of undisturbed sleep a night, so that your body has a chance to work the way it should and you have the energy to get through the day.

Existing Medical Conditions

There are many medical problems and medications taken to treat medical issues that make weight loss difficult or cause weight gain. For example, if you have a hormonal disorder such as PCOS or hypothyroidism, you might have difficulty losing weight. Be sure to look at the labels on any medication you take, to see if weight gain is listed as a side effect. Sometimes there are no effective alternative medicines for your ailment, but it is prudent to at least ask your doctor for options. If you are doing everything right with respect to creating a positive environment for weight loss and still simply cannot drop pounds, then consult your medical professional to see if there might be an underlying medical cause.

Eating Too Many Nuts or Too Much Fruit

When people start a new diet, they sometimes initially stick to familiar dishes that fit the parameters of the diet. This often means nuts and fruit. Nuts are a great source of nutrients and protein, but they are also very high in fat. Having nut butters for breakfast, a handful of nuts for a snack, pad thai with a spicy nut sauce for lunch, and cashew-crusted fish for dinner will make you gain weight. Nuts should be an accent to provide texture and taste rather than a staple of your meals. Fruit is also a tricky area for some people. Fruit is healthy and fiber-packed and satisfies a sweet tooth. But fruit is also high in natural sugars, which should not be the base of your diet. Balance and planning are key to reaching and maintaining a healthy weight.

PART FOUR

150 Paleo Recipes

CHAPTER TWELVE

30 Paleo Breakfasts

- Mint-Infused Melon Fruit Salad
- Crunchy Almond Granola
- Paleo "Oatmeal"
- Vanilla Quinoa Cereal
- Quinoa Porridge
- Egg White Scramble
- Italian Vegetable Frittata
- Mediterranean Vegetable Frittata
- Zucchini-Asparagus Chicken Frittata
- Swiss Chard-Chicken Omelet
- Roasted Red Pepper-Sausage Omelet
- Eggs Florentine
- Portobello Mushroom Eggs Florentine
- Creamy Baked Eggs
- Baked Eggs in Salsa

- Sweet Potato Quiche
- Breakfast Pudding
- Sweet Potato Hash
- Paleo Breakfast Sausage
- Breakfast Stir-Fry
- Tender Almond Pancakes
- Banana-Vanilla Pancakes
- Spiced Banana-Coconut Waffles
- Orange French Toast
- Banana French Toast
- Apple Paleo Muffins
- Blueberry Crumble Muffins
- Chocolate Chip-Strawberry Muffins
- Orange-Cranberry Scones
- Chocolate-Raspberry Donuts

Mint-Infused Melon Fruit Salad

This salad is refreshing and sweet and provides a great deal of energy for your busy day. The colors are gorgeous and the different textures make for an interesting culinary experience. Use ripe but firm fruit for the best results, and be sure to let the salad stand for an hour so the mint has time to meld with the other ingredients.

½ small cantaloupe, peeled, seeded, and cut into ½-inch chunks

¼ small honeydew melon, peeled, seeded, and cut into ½-inch chunks

½ pint fresh blueberries

½ pint ripe strawberries, hulled and sliced

1 large Asian pear, cut into ½-inch pieces

½ small English cucumber with the skin on, diced

½ cup freshly squeezed orange juice

¼ cup julienned fresh mint

1. In a large bowl, toss together all of the ingredients except the orange juice and mint.

2. In a small bowl, whisk together the orange juice and mint, and pour over fruit.

3. Let stand for at least 1 hour, tossing several times to coat fruit, then transfer to 4 serving bowls and serve.

Crunchy Almond Granola

MAKES 8 SERVINGS

If you are a cereal lover, this granola will be your new favorite. It is exceptional and easy to make in large quantities. It freezes well in freezer bags or sealable containers. This is a great recipe to make with kids because you can mix it all up with your hands and the measurements don't have to be precise.

1 cup almond meal, lightly packed and dried in a 300-degree oven for 15 minutes
½ cup shredded unsweetened coconut
½ cup sunflower seeds
½ cup slivered almonds
¼ cup pistachios
2 tablespoons sesame seeds
1 teaspoon ground cinnamon
½ teaspoon sea salt
¼ cup coconut oil, melted
½ cup honey
1 cup dried cranberries

1. Preheat the oven to 325°F.

2. In a large bowl, toss together the dried almond meal, coconut, sunflower seeds, almonds, pistachios, sesame seeds, cinnamon, and salt until well mixed.

3. In a small bowl, whisk together the coconut oil and honey until blended.

4. Add the honey mixture to the large bowl. Using your hands, mix the wet ingredients into the dry ingredients until evenly coated, about 5 minutes.

5. Transfer the mixture to 2 baking sheets and place in the oven.

6. Bake, stirring frequently, until the granola is evenly browned and dry, about 1 hour.

7. Remove from the oven and allow to cool.

8. Break up the granola and add the dried cranberries.

Paleo "Oatmeal"

Sometimes a bowl of warm cereal is the best way to start a cool fall morning, and this "oatmeal" fits the bill. It is nutty and slightly chewy while being sweet from the banana and fresh berries. You can substitute different nuts and nut butters in this recipe for other variations and flavors. You must cook this dish for at least 5 minutes to ensure that the eggs are completely cooked.

½ cup almonds

½ cup pecans

¼ cup ground flaxseed

1 teaspoon ground cinnamon

¼ teaspoon ground ginger

¼ teaspoon ground nutmeg

5 large eggs

½ cup almond milk, plus more for topping

2 large ripe bananas, mashed

2 tablespoons almond butter

2 cups blueberries, for topping

1. Place the nuts, flaxseed, and spices in a food processor and pulse until it resembles coarse crumbs. Transfer to a large saucepan and set aside.

2. In a small bowl, stir together the eggs and almond milk until thoroughly combined and thick.

3. Add the mashed banana and almond butter to the nut mixture in the saucepan and whisk until blended.

4. Stir the wet ingredients into the nut mixture and place over medium heat.

5. Cook the resulting nut mixture, stirring constantly, until it is thick and the eggs are completely cooked, 5 to 7 minutes.

6. Sprinkle with blueberries and serve with a little more almond milk.

Vanilla Quinoa Cereal

MAKES 4 SERVINGS

Quinoa is a pseudograin that some people do not include in Paleo eating plans, but it meets the Paleo criteria because it is actually a seed. It is a nice choice for many different dishes, like this creamy cereal. Vanilla beans are also wonderful in this dish, especially if you infuse the liquids beforehand by heating them with a vanilla bean split down the middle. Simply scrape out the seeds and reserve the bean for another use.

2 cups water
2 cups unsweetened vanilla almond milk
2 cups uncooked quinoa, washed and picked over
Pinch of sea salt
1 teaspoon pure vanilla extract
2 tablespoons maple syrup
1 cup blueberries, for topping
2 tablespoons slivered almonds, for topping

1. In a medium saucepan, combine the water, almond milk, quinoa, salt, and vanilla.

2. Cover and cook over medium heat until simmering; reduce the heat and simmer until quinoa is done.

3. Add the maple syrup and a dash more almond milk to create the desired texture.

4. Top with blueberries and almonds.

Quinoa Porridge

This porridge will remind you of convenient packages of instant oatmeal because it is quite sweet due to the dates. If you want it less sweet, reduce the number of dates used in the recipe. Dates are perfect for breakfast because they are quick sources of energy for several hours after consuming them. Soak the dates in the almond milk for 1 hour before puréeing the mixture to soften them.

2 cups plain almond milk, plus a splash for serving
6 dates
1 cup quinoa, soaked and rinsed
1 teaspoon ground cinnamon
¼ teaspoon ground ginger
¼ teaspoon ground nutmeg
Pinch of ground cloves

1. Blend the almond milk and dates in a blender until smooth.

2. Place the remaining ingredients in a saucepan with the almond-milk mixture and cook over medium heat until boiling.

3. Reduce the heat to low and simmer, stirring, until most of the liquid has been absorbed, about 15 minutes.

4. Serve with a little more almond milk.

Egg White Scramble

Though this dish uses some very humble ingredients, it's so spectacular that a four-star restaurant could serve it with pride. Not only is it tasty, but the snowy eggs, vibrant greens, and deep red tomatoes are visually stunning. You can substitute other greens, such as watercress or Swiss chard, for the spinach in this recipe with great results.

Olive oil cooking spray
½ small sweet onion, finely chopped
1 teaspoon minced garlic
1 small yellow bell pepper, seeded and chopped
1 cup egg whites (about 10 egg whites)
2 cups shredded baby spinach
3 plum tomatoes, seeded and diced
Sea salt and cracked black pepper to taste
2 tablespoons grated vegan cheese, for topping
2 tablespoons chopped basil, for topping

1. Lightly spray a large skillet with olive oil spray and place over medium-high heat.

2. Add the onion, garlic, and bell pepper and sauté until the onions are translucent.

3. In a medium bowl, whisk together the egg whites, spinach, and tomatoes until well combined.

4. Add the egg mixture to skillet and scramble until dry, about 4 minutes.

5. Season with salt and pepper to taste.

6. Serve topped with vegan cheese and chopped basil.

Italian Vegetable Frittata

MAKES 4 SERVINGS

Artichoke hearts play a pivotal role in this festive frittata. These tasty flower buds are a great source of antioxidants and fiber. Artichoke hearts can decrease the risk of certain types of cancer and cardiovascular disease. Try to find hearts packed in water if you don't want to steam or blanch fresh artichokes.

2 cups egg whites (about 20 egg whites)

½ cup freshly shredded vegan cheese

2 tablespoons chopped fresh basil

Cracked black pepper to taste

1 teaspoon olive oil

1 teaspoon minced garlic

2 scallions, finely chopped

½ cup canned quartered artichoke hearts, drained

1 cup halved cherry or grape tomatoes

1 ounce diced, lean nitrate-free ham

1. Preheat oven to broil.

2. In a medium bowl, whisk together the egg whites, cheese, basil, and pepper; set aside.

3. Place a large ovenproof skillet over medium-high heat; add the olive oil. Add the garlic and scallions and sauté for 1 minute.

4. Add the artichoke hearts, tomatoes, and ham and sauté for 3 to 4 minutes.

5. Remove the skillet from heat and pour in the egg mixture.

6. Return the skillet to the heat, cover, and cook without stirring for 10 to 12 minutes, or until the egg mixture is set in center.

7. Remove from the heat and place skillet under the broiler for 1 minute or until the top is lightly browned.

8. Transfer to a serving plate and cut into quarters. Serve hot or at room temperature.

Mediterranean Vegetable Frittata

This dish will call up visions of sun-drenched beaches, azure skies, and white balconies because it combines traditional Mediterranean ingredients. Zucchini, garlic, peppers, and tomatoes add a robust texture and taste to the eggs. Serving this frittata in thick wedges adds to its rustic appeal.

2 teaspoons coconut oil

½ red bell pepper, seeded and diced

½ yellow bell pepper, seeded and diced

½ small red onion, peeled and diced

1 small green zucchini, diced

2 teaspoons minced garlic

2 small tomatoes, seeded and chopped

10 large eggs, beaten with a dash of sea salt and cracked black pepper

2 teaspoons minced fresh thyme, for topping

1. Preheat oven to low broil.

2. Place a large ovenproof skillet over medium-high heat; add the oil.

3. When the skillet is hot, add the bell peppers, onion, zucchini, and the garlic.

4. Cook, stirring, until the vegetables are tender, about 5 minutes.

5. Add the tomatoes and cook until the liquid evaporates, about 5 minutes.

6. Reduce the heat to low and add the eggs to the skillet.

7. Cover and cook for about 15 minutes, or until the eggs are set.

8. Place the skillet in preheated oven under the broiler and bake for about 2 minutes.

9. Invert onto a serving plate and top with thyme. Serve hot or at room temperature.

Zucchini-Asparagus Chicken Frittata

MAKES 4 SERVINGS

At first glance, frittatas might seem to be the same as omelets because their ingredients are pretty much identical. The difference is that frittatas usually have the filling mixed into the eggs, and omelets have the eggs folded over the filling. If you want to make perfect frittatas, invest in a cast-iron skillet that can go right into the oven.

1 teaspoon olive oil

½ small green zucchini, diced

½ small yellow zucchini, diced

1 small red bell pepper, cut into thin strips

½ small red onion, finely chopped

12 fresh asparagus spears, blanched and chopped into 1-inch-long pieces

1 cup diced cooked chicken

½ cup shredded vegan cheese

2 cups egg whites (about 20 egg whites)

½ cup coconut milk

1 tablespoon chopped fresh basil

2 tablespoons arrowroot starch

Sea salt and cracked black pepper to taste

1. Preheat the oven to 350°F and lightly oil a 9 × 9-inch baking dish.

2. In a large skillet, heat the oil and sauté the zucchini, red pepper, and onion until tender.

3. Transfer the vegetables to the prepared baking dish and spread out evenly. Add the asparagus and chicken and sprinkle with half of the vegan cheese.

4. In a medium bowl, whisk together the egg whites, coconut milk, arrowroot starch, basil, and black pepper until well combined.

5. Pour the egg mixture over the vegetables in the baking dish.

6. Bake, uncovered, for about 35 minutes or until set.

7. Sprinkle the finished frittata with the remaining vegan cheese and let stand for 10 minutes. Serve warm or at room temperature.

Swiss Chard-Chicken Omelet

MAKES 3 SERVINGS

Chicken might seem like a strange choice for breakfast, but since it combines beautifully with the greens and cheese in the recipe, why not bend the culinary rules? Chicken is a staple of the Paleo diet, so cook a few chicken breasts at a time and you will always have some on hand for salads and omelets.

1 teaspoon olive oil
2 packed cups chopped green or red Swiss chard
1 small sweet onion, chopped
1 teaspoon minced garlic
1 cup cooked diced chicken
3 cups egg whites
½ cup vegan cheese
Olive oil cooking spray
Sea salt
Cracked black pepper to taste
Hot pepper sauce to taste

1. Heat a large nonstick skillet over medium-high heat; add the oil.

2. Add the chard, onion, and garlic and sauté, stirring often, until tender.

3. Remove the mixture to a small bowl and add chicken.

4. Wipe the skillet clean.

5. In a medium bowl, combine egg whites and vegan cheese.

6. Lightly spray the skillet with olive oil cooking spray and place over high heat.

7. Pour in the egg mixture and lightly shake the skillet to spread eggs evenly.

8. After about a minute, tilt the skillet to allow the eggs to flow to edges.

9. Keep tilting the skillet until eggs are firm and the underside is lightly browned.

10. Flip the omelet over to cook other side, then remove from the heat.

11. Spoon the chard mixture into the omelet and fold in half.

12. Divide the omelet into three wedges and slide onto plates.

13. Season with salt, pepper, and hot sauce if desired. Serve immediately.

Roasted Red Pepper-Sausage Omelet

MAKES 2 SERVINGS

Roasted peppers have a unique flavor that is completely different from raw peppers. For the easiest way to create perfect skinless roasted peppers, place the whole peppers in a heavy skillet over high heat and keep turning them until the skin is blistered on all sides. Remove the peppers from the pan and place them in a stainless steel bowl covered tightly with plastic wrap. The peppers will steam their own skins loose, and you'll be able to pull them off easily after about 10 minutes.

1 tablespoon coconut oil
4 large eggs beaten with sea salt and black pepper
1 roasted red bell pepper, skinned, seeded, and diced
4 nitrate-free sausages, cooked and thinly sliced
½ cup halved cherry tomatoes

1. Place a medium nonstick skillet over medium-high heat; add the oil.

2. When skillet is hot, add half the eggs and cook until just starting to set.

3. Sprinkle half of the peppers, sausage, and cherry tomatoes over half of the omelet.

4. Continue to cook until the eggs are set, then fold in half.

5. Slide the omelet onto a plate and repeat for the second omelet. Serve immediately.

Eggs Florentine

MAKES 3 SERVINGS

Spinach and eggs combine beautifully. Spinach is a wonderful source of important nutrients, such as vitamin K, vitamin A, manganese, and folate. By including spinach in this breakfast scramble, you are starting the day out right.

Olive oil cooking spray
½ cup chopped red onion
1 cup sliced white mushrooms
8 large egg whites
1 teaspoon minced garlic
1 teaspoon nutmeg
½ cup plain almond milk
1 cup shredded baby spinach
½ cup grated low-fat vegan cheese
Sea salt and cracked black pepper to taste
Chopped parsley, for garnish

1. Spray a large skillet with olive oil spray and place over medium-high heat.

2. Add the onion and mushrooms and sauté until the vegetables are tender.

3. In a medium bowl, whisk together the eggs, garlic, nutmeg, almond milk, spinach, and seasonings.

4. Pour the egg mixture into skillet and allow to set slightly.

5. Top with the vegan cheese and cook until the eggs are cooked through. Divide into thirds and top with parsley. Serve immediately.

Portobello Mushroom Eggs Florentine

MAKES 2 SERVINGS

This is a stacked breakfast that features meaty portobello mushrooms instead of the usual English muffin base. Mushrooms are a great source of phytochemicals, which are crucial for good health. They also contain powerful antioxidants such as L-ergothioneine, which is not destroyed by cooking, unlike some nutrients in other foods.

1 tablespoon coconut oil

4 large portobello mushrooms, stems removed

4 large eggs

4 slices nitrate-free smoked ham

1 cup packed baby spinach leaves

Sea salt and cracked black pepper to taste

Pinch of paprika

1. Place a large skillet over medium heat; add the oil.

2. Place the mushroom caps in the skillet and cook until softened on both sides, turning once, about 3 minutes.

3. Set aside on a plate with gills facing up.

4. In a saucepan, poach the eggs in lightly simmering water with a splash of vinegar until they are set, about 4 to 5 minutes. Remove the eggs with a slotted spoon and place on paper towels to drain.

5. Place 2 portobello mushrooms on each plate and top with sliced ham.

6. Add a handful of spinach leaves to each and place a poached egg over the spinach.

7. Season to taste with salt and pepper, sprinkle with a little paprika, and serve.

Creamy Baked Eggs

MAKES 2 SERVINGS

The leeks, cream, and hint of garlic create a decadent dish that would be at home on an elegant hotel menu or served poolside at a resort. Take the time to clean your leeks very well because they are always gritty. The best way to clean leeks is to slice them and place them in a full sink of water or large bowl. Swish them around with your hands and then let them sit for at least 15 minutes in the water. The leeks will float and the dirt will sink to the bottom. Scoop them out with a slotted spoon and pat dry to use.

1 teaspoon coconut oil
1 teaspoon minced garlic
4 leeks, white and light green parts only, washed and washed and thinly sliced
4 cups dark leafy greens (spinach, beet greens, or Swiss chard), thinly sliced
Juice of one small lemon
½ cup coconut milk
4 eggs, at room temperature
Sea salt and cracked black pepper to taste

1. Preheat the oven to 400°F.

2. Place a large skillet over medium-high heat; add the oil.

3. Add the garlic and leeks and sauté for about 3 minutes, stirring occasionally, until softened.

4. Add greens and sauté until wilted, about 5 minutes.

5. Add the lemon juice and season with salt and pepper to taste.

6. Sauté for 1 minute.

7. Add the coconut milk and simmer, stirring, until the liquid has almost evaporated.

8. Spoon the mixture into 4 individual ramekins or a shallow casserole dish, making 4 wells for the eggs.

9. Crack an egg into each well, taking care not to break the yolks.

10. Bake for 10 to 15 minutes, or until the whites are set.

Baked Eggs in Salsa

MAKES 2 SERVINGS

This dish will remind you of huevos rancheros without the beans. Beans are not allowed on the Paleo diet, so these spicy eggs are a great alternative. Jalapeño peppers are not overly hot and they contain capsaicin, which has been linked to reducing types of cancer and cardiovascular disease. If you want your dish hotter, add more jalapeño or a dash of dried red chili flakes.

1 teaspoon coconut oil

½ sweet onion, peeled and finely chopped

1 teaspoon minced garlic

4 tomatoes, seeded and diced

1 small red bell pepper, seeded and finely chopped

1 jalapeño pepper, finely chopped

Sea salt and cracked black pepper to taste

4 large eggs

¼ cup grated aged vegan cheddar cheese

1 green onion, finely chopped

look for salsa

1. Preheat oven to 350°F.

2. Place a skillet over medium-high heat; add the oil.

3. Add the onion and garlic and sauté until the onion is translucent, about 3 minutes.

4. Add the tomatoes, red pepper, and jalapeño pepper and sauté for about 5 minutes.

5. Season with salt and pepper to taste and spoon the tomato mixture into a casserole dish.

6. Using the back of a spoon, make 4 deep wells in the tomato mixture. Crack an egg into each well and bake for about 10 to 15 minutes or until the eggs are firm.

7. Sprinkle with grated cheese and put the dish back into oven for about 3 minutes, until the cheese is melted.

8. Sprinkle with the green onions and serve.

Sweet Potato Quiche

This quiche has a surprise crust made completely of meat. The trick to making a great crust is to use lean sausage that will not shrink too much in the oven and to pour off any extra fat. You can buy loose sausage meat in packages, but an even better idea is to make your own sausage so you know exactly what is in it.

1 pound nitrate-free breakfast sausage, squeezed out of casings

1 teaspoon reserved fat from cooking sausage

1 cup diced sweet onion

1 small sweet potato, peeled and diced

1½ teaspoons minced garlic

2 packed cups fresh spinach

5 large eggs, whisked

Sea salt and cracked black pepper to taste

Pinch of cayenne pepper

1. Preheat oven to 375°F.

2. Press the sausage evenly into a 9-inch pie plate so it covers the bottom and sides.

3. Place the pie plate on a baking sheet and put into the preheated oven.

4. Bake until the meat is just completely cooked through. Remove from the oven and pour off all the fat, reserving 1 teaspoon.

5. Add reserved fat to a large skillet placed over medium-high heat.

6. Add the onion, sweet potato, and garlic and sauté until potatoes are cooked through, about 5 minutes.

7. Add the spinach and cook, covered, until wilted, about 1 minute. Transfer the potato mixture to a bowl and cool.

8. When the potato mixture is cool, stir in the eggs, salt, pepper, and cayenne.

9. Pour egg mixture into meat crust and bake for about 25 minutes or until eggs are set.

10. Cool slightly and serve.

Breakfast Pudding

MAKES 4 SERVINGS

Roasted squash has a smooth, sweet, and almost nutty taste that is very satisfying for breakfast. If you don't have much time in the morning, you can roast the squash the day before and reheat it with the rest of the ingredients. Simply remove the skin while the squash is warm and place the flesh in a sealed container in the fridge until you need it.

Coconut oil, for baking sheet
1 small butternut squash
⅓ cup shredded unsweetened coconut
2 teaspoons ground cinnamon
1 teaspoon ground ginger
¼ cup maple syrup, for topping
¼ cup chopped pecans, for topping

1. Preheat the oven to 400°F. Lightly grease a baking sheet with the coconut oil.

2. Cut the squash in half and scoop out the seeds.

3. Place the squash, cut-side down, on the prepared baking sheet and bake for about 1 hour or until the squash is very tender.

4. Let the squash cool for about 10 minutes, then scoop the flesh into a saucepan.

5. Add the coconut milk, shredded coconut, cinnamon, and ginger. Mash with a potato masher until smooth.

6. Heat on low until the pudding is the desired temperature.

7. Serve topped with a drizzle of maple syrup and a sprinkle of chopped pecans.

Sweet Potato Hash

MAKES 4 SERVINGS

Starchy vegetables are in the gray area for the Paleo diet, but according to Loren Cordain, the founder of Paleo, sweet potatoes can be eaten in moderation. To make this a whole meal, hollow out sections in the cooked hash and cook sunny-side up eggs right in the same pan.

1 tablespoon extra virgin olive oil
½ small sweet onion, peeled and chopped
4 large sweet potatoes, grated
½ teaspoon chopped fresh thyme
Sea salt
Cracked black pepper to taste

1. Place a large skillet over medium-high heat; add the oil.

2. Add the onion and saute until it begins to caramelize, about 5 minutes.

3. Add the sweet potato and cook until browned.

4. Remove from the heat and season with thyme, salt, and pepper.

5. Serve with your favorite eggs or some crispy uncured bacon.

Paleo Breakfast Sausage

MAKES 16 SAUSAGE PATTIES

Homemade sausage is easier to make than most people think and contains none of the harmful nitrates and additives found in much commercially prepared sausage. You can use your favorite herbs instead of the ones here for different flavors, such as a hint of chili for Italian sausage. This recipe freezes well, so double the batch and put the extras away for future meals.

1½ teaspoons sea salt

1 teaspoon cracked black pepper

1 teaspoon smoked sweet paprika

1 teaspoon smoked hot paprika

1 teaspoon dried oregano

1 teaspoon rubbed sage

2 pounds lean ground pork

1 tablespoon coconut oil

1. In a large bowl, whisk together the salt, pepper, paprikas, and herbs until well mixed.

2. Add the ground pork and mix together until the herbs are incorporated.

3. Form the pork mixture into 16 equal balls and flatten into patties.

4. Place a skillet over medium heat; add the oil.

5. When the skillet is hot, cook the patties in batches until browned and cooked through, about 5 minutes per side.

6. Serve with your favorite eggs.

Breakfast Stir-Fry

MAKES 3 SERVINGS

Bacon is one food that some people do not include in their Paleo diet plan, but others do. Bacon is not a part of the original Paleo diet, so if you are going to eat it, avoid heavily processed products. There are some very tasty brands on the market that are not cured and packed with nitrates, such as those by Applegate Farms or 365 brand Applewood Smoked Uncured Pork Bacon at Whole Foods.

10 uncured nitrate-free bacon slices, diced
1 small sweet onion, diced
2 medium cooked sweet potatoes, peeled and diced
1 red bell pepper, seeded and diced
1 cup green beans, cut in half
Sea salt and cracked black pepper to taste
1 tablespoon chopped chives, for topping

1. Place a large skillet over medium-high heat and sauté bacon until completely cooked. Remove the cooked bacon with a slotted spoon and drain the fat, reserving 1 tablespoon.

2. Wipe the pan clean, add the reserved bacon fat, and set over medium heat.

3. Add the onion and sauté until translucent, about 5 minutes.

4. Add the sweet potatoes and sauté until they start to brown.

5. Add the red pepper and green beans and cook, stirring constantly, until the pepper softens and the green beans are crisp-tender.

6. Remove the pan from the heat and add the bacon.

7. Season with salt and pepper and serve topped with chives.

Tender Almond Pancakes

MAKES 4 SERVINGS

Pancakes are a perfect Sunday morning breakfast with family or an easy grab-and-go snack eaten cold during the week if you make extra. The carbonated water provides a nice rise, but you can substitute plain water or almond milk if you wish. Make sure the skillet is not overly hot or the pancakes will stick and brown too much.

2 cups almond flour
¼ cup coconut flour
½ teaspoon ground nutmeg
¼ teaspoon ground cinnamon
¼ teaspoon sea salt
1 cup unsweetened applesauce
4 large eggs, lightly beaten
½ cup carbonated water
Coconut oil, for greasing the skillet
Freshly cut fruit, for topping
Sliced almonds, for topping

1. In a large bowl, combine the almond flour, coconut flour, nutmeg, cinnamon, and salt until very well mixed.

2. Make a well in the center of the dry ingredients and add the applesauce, eggs, and carbonated water. Mix together with a fork until combined.

3. In a skillet set over medium heat, heat about 1 teaspoon of coconut oil.

4. Add about ½ cup batter to the hot skillet and spread out slightly with the back of a spoon.

5. Flip the pancake over when bubbles start appearing on the top. Cook until both sides are golden and the pancake is cooked through, about 30 more seconds.

6. Add a little more oil to skillet and repeat with remaining batter.

7. Top with fresh fruit and sliced almonds.

Banana-Vanilla Pancakes

MAKES 4 SERVINGS

Vanilla is a lovely complement to the ripe bananas in this recipe, and using a vanilla bean creates even richer flavor. Vanilla beans contain some B complex vitamins and traces of many minerals such as calcium, potassium, iron, and zinc. This means vanilla can help regulate the body's metabolism and normalize heart rate and blood pressure.

3 large eggs
2 large ripe bananas
Seeds from 1 vanilla bean
1 teaspoon pure vanilla extract
3 tablespoons coconut flour
¼ teaspoon baking soda
¼ teaspoon ground cinnamon
Pinch of sea salt
Coconut oil, for greasing the skillet
Fresh fruit or maple syrup, for topping

1. Place the eggs, bananas, vanilla seeds, and vanilla extract in a food processor and pulse until very smooth.

2. Add the coconut flour, baking soda, cinnamon, and salt and pulse until smooth.

3. Let sit for about 10 minutes so the coconut flour can absorb the liquid. Pulse again a couple of times.

4. Place a large skillet over medium heat and brush with a bit of coconut oil.

5. When the skillet is hot, add about ¼ cup of the batter and cook until bubbles appear on the top, about 3 minutes.

6. Flip the pancake and cook until browned on the second side and cooked through.

7. Repeat until all batter is used.

8. Serve topped with fresh fruit or a drizzle of real maple syrup.

Spiced Banana-Coconut Waffles

MAKES 4 LARGE SERVINGS

You will need a waffle iron to make these crunchy beauties. Coconut, banana, and maple syrup all combine to create a tropical breakfast treat. You can make a double batch of waffles and freeze the leftovers to pop in the toaster anytime for a convenient meal. You can also top these waffles with a few spoonfuls of homemade applesauce for something more filling.

Coconut oil for the waffle iron
2 large ripe bananas
2 large eggs
¼ cup coconut milk
¼ cup maple syrup
2 teaspoons coconut oil
1 cup shredded unsweetened coconut
1 cup almond meal
4 teaspoons arrowroot powder
1 teaspoon baking soda
1 teaspoon ground cinnamon
½ teaspoon ground nutmeg
Pinch of ground cloves
Pinch of sea salt
Sliced ripe bananas, for topping
Pecan pieces, for topping
Maple syrup, for topping, if desired

1. Preheat waffle iron and lightly grease with oil.

2. Place the bananas, eggs, coconut milk, maple syrup, and coconut oil in a blender or food processor and blend until smooth.

3. Transfer the banana mixture to a large bowl; set aside.

4. In a medium bowl, stir together the coconut, almond meal, arrowroot, baking soda, spices, and salt until well combined.

5. Add the dry ingredients to the wet ingredients and stir to combine.

6. Pour the batter by half cupfuls into the preheated waffle iron and cook according to the manufacturer's directions.

7. Serve topped with bananas, pecans, and a little maple syrup, if desired.

Paleo for Beginners

Orange French Toast

This dish has a lovely orange taste and scent that combine perfectly with multi-grain Paleo bread. You can either make your own or buy a good-quality bread. Take the time to wash the orange thoroughly before zesting it, to remove any harmful pesticides or contaminants on the skin.

Olive oil cooking spray
1 large egg, beaten
1 egg white, beaten
½ cup almond milk
1 teaspoon pure vanilla extract
Pinch of ground cinnamon
Juice and zest of 1 orange
8 slices Paleo bread

1. Spray a large baking sheet with cooking spray.

2. Preheat oven to 450°F.

3. In a medium bowl, whisk together the egg, egg white, almond milk, vanilla, cinnamon, zest, and juice.

4. Dip the bread slices in the egg mixture and place side by side on prepared baking sheet.

5. Bake for about 5 minutes, or until the bread is golden, then flip bread over and bake for 5 minutes or until golden brown on the other side. Serve immediately.

Banana French Toast

MAKES 4 TO 5 SERVINGS

This sweet, decadent dish should be your special brunch dish for loved ones and company. Make sure the banana bread is completely cool before slicing it or the French toast will crumble. You might want to make an extra loaf of banana bread to enjoy later; it is exceptional.

For the banana bread:

Coconut oil for greasing the pan

3 ripe bananas, mashed

3 large eggs

¼ cup honey

3 tablespoons coconut oil

2 tablespoons coconut cream (the thick layer at the top of a can of coconut milk)

1 ½ cups almond flour

3 tablespoons tapioca flour

2 tablespoons unsweetened shredded coconut

1 teaspoon baking powder

1 teaspoon ground cinnamon

½ cup pecan pieces

For the French toast:

2 large eggs

½ cup canned coconut milk, shaken

1 teaspoon pure vanilla extract

2 tablespoons coconut oil, for skillet

Fresh fruit or maple syrup for serving

Make the banana bread:

1. Preheat the oven to 325°F.

2. Grease a 9 × 5-inch loaf pan with a bit of the coconut oil. Line the bottom of the pan with parchment paper and grease the parchment.

3. In a large bowl, beat together the bananas, eggs, honey, coconut oil, and coconut cream with a hand mixer until well mixed.

4. In a smaller bowl, combine all of the remaining ingredients, except for the pecans, and mix well.

continued ▶

st continued ▶

...ngredients to the wet ingredients and beat to combine.

6. Spoon the batter into the prepared loaf pan and smooth the surface with the back of a spoon. Sprinkle the top with pecans.

7. Bake for 45 minutes or until a toothpick inserted into the center comes out clean.

8. Let cool for 5 to 10 minutes and remove from the pan. Place on a wire cooling rack. Cool completely before using for French toast.

Make the French toast:

1. In a medium bowl whisk together the eggs, coconut milk, and vanilla.

2. Place a large skillet over medium-high heat; add about ½ teaspoon of the coconut oil.

3. Cut the banana bread into 8 to 10 equal slices and dip them into the egg mixture, gently shaking off the excess liquid.

4. Place the slices in the hot skillet and cook for about 4 minutes, until both sides are golden brown, turning once.

5. Continue cooking until all of the bread is used. Serve plain, with fresh fruit, or with a drizzle of maple syrup.

Apple Paleo Muffins

MAKES 9 MUFFINS

Apples are perfect for many recipes because people usually have them on hand. Apples can help prevent several cancers, including lung, breast, liver, and colon cancer. They also help minimize the symptoms of asthma and support good bone health. These muffins can jump-start your day.

Coconut oil, for greasing the muffin cups
2 cups almond flour
½ teaspoon baking soda
Pinch of sea salt
3 large eggs
¼ cup maple syrup
2 tablespoons coconut oil, melted
2 teaspoons fresh lemon juice
1 teaspoon pure vanilla extract
1 cup chopped, peeled apples

1. Preheat the oven to 325°F.

2. Use coconut oil to lightly grease 9 muffin cups. Line the bottoms of cups with parchment. Grease the parchment and set cups aside.

3. In a large bowl, stir together the almond flour, baking soda, and salt until well combined.

4. In a small bowl, whisk together the eggs, maple syrup, coconut oil, lemon juice, and vanilla.

5. Add the wet ingredients to the dry ingredients and stir until just mixed.

6. Add apple pieces and stir.

7. Spoon the batter into muffin cups and bake for about 20 minutes, or until a toothpick inserted into the center comes out clean.

8. Remove from the oven, cool in the muffin tin for 5 minutes on a rack, and then turn out onto the rack to cool. Serve warm or at room temperature.

Blueberry Crumble Muffins

MAKES 12 MUFFINS

These tender muffins have many ingredients and might seem complicated to make, but they are worth the effort. They are also lovely with ripe peaches or even plums for a rich, exotic taste. Peel the stone fruit and cube, and add the same quantity used for the blueberries.

For the blueberry muffins:

2 cups almond flour

¼ teaspoon baking soda

⅛ teaspoon sea salt

1 cup full-fat coconut milk

2 large eggs

¼ cup honey

¼ cup coconut oil, melted

¾ cup fresh blueberries

For the crumble topping:

½ cup chilled coconut oil

Pinch of salt

1 tablespoon coconut flour

2 teaspoons almond meal

1 teaspoon cinnamon

Pinch of ground nutmeg

1 teaspoon pure vanilla extract

2 tablespoons maple syrup

½ cup toasted shredded unsweetened coconut

⅓ cup slivered almonds

Make the blueberry muffins:

1. Preheat the oven to 350°F.

2. Line a 12-cup muffin tin with paper liners.

3. In a large bowl, stir together the almond flour, baking soda, and salt until well mixed.

4. In a medium bowl stir together the coconut milk, eggs, honey, and coconut oil until well blended.

5. Add the wet to the dry ingredients and stir to combine.

6. Carefully fold the blueberries into batter.

7. Spoon the batter into the muffin cups; set aside.

For the crumble topping:

1. Place all ingredients in a food processor and pulse until mixture resembles coarse crumbs.

2. Top muffins evenly with crumble.

3. Bake muffins for 20 to 25 minutes or until golden brown.

4. Let muffins cool completely before removing from pan.

Chocolate Chip-Strawberry Muffins

These treats are similar to the baked products you can find in high-end coffee shops. They are chocolaty, tender, and studded with jewel-like berries. You can also add a tablespoon of good-quality cocoa powder to the batter to create a double-chocolate treat. Dark chocolate is actually very good for you because it contains antioxidants and is heart-friendly.

Coconut oil, for greasing the muffin tin
2 cups almond flour
½ cup mini dark chocolate chips
½ teaspoon baking soda
Pinch of sea salt
3 large eggs
¼ cup maple syrup or honey
2 tablespoons coconut oil, melted
1 tablespoon fresh lemon juice
1 teaspoon pure vanilla extract
1 cup fresh strawberries, trimmed and sliced

1. Preheat the oven to 325°F.

2. Lightly grease 9 muffin cups with coconut oil. Line the bottom of the cups with parchment paper. Grease the parchment.

3. In a large bowl, stir together the almond flour, chocolate chips, baking soda, and salt.

4. In a small bowl, whisk together the eggs, maple syrup, coconut oil, lemon juice, and vanilla until well blended.

5. Add the wet ingredients to the dry ingredients and stir to combine.

6. Fold in the strawberries and spoon the batter into the prepared muffin cups.

7. Bake for 20 to 25 minutes or until a toothpick inserted into the center of one muffin comes out clean.

8. Remove from the oven, let cool on a rack for 5 minutes in the muffin tin, then turn out onto the rack. Cool and serve.

Orange-Cranberry Scones

MAKES 8 SCONES

Scones are very traditional English breakfast biscuits that are served with cream and berries. These orange-scented scones are delicate and have a tender crumb, so you won't miss the clotted cream. The dried cranberries add a lovely tartness and texture, so do not substitute anything else if possible.

3 cups almond flour

1 cup dried cranberries

2 teaspoons orange zest

1 teaspoon baking soda

⅛ teaspoon sea salt

2 large eggs

2 tablespoons honey

2 tablespoons fresh orange juice

1. Preheat the oven to 325°F. Line a baking sheet with parchment paper.

2. In a large bowl, stir together the almond flour, cranberries, orange zest, baking soda, and salt until well combined.

3. In a small bowl, whisk together the eggs, honey, and orange juice.

4. Pour the wet ingredients into the dry ingredients and stir until just combined.

5. Divide the batter into 8 large balls and drop onto the prepared baking sheet. Flatten the balls until they are about 1 inch thick.

6. Bake for 20 to 25 minutes or until golden brown.

7. Cool and serve.

Chocolate-Raspberry Donuts

MAKES 6 DONUTS

Did you ever think you would be eating donuts while following a Paleo diet plan? With a donut pan you can create these dense treats easily—and they are Paleo! Donut pans can be found in most kitchen or baking supplies stores and online. You can create a simple chocolate glaze by melting a little dark chocolate with coconut oil and drizzling it over the cooled donuts.

Coconut oil, for greasing the pan

2 cups fine almond meal

¼ cup unsweetened cocoa powder

2 teaspoons coconut flour

1 teaspoon baking soda

Pinch of sea salt

4 large eggs

¼ cup honey

¼ cup coconut oil

1 teaspoon pure vanilla extract

1 cup fresh raspberries

⅓ cup dark chocolate chips

1. Preheat the oven to 350°F. Lightly grease a donut pan with coconut oil.

2. In a large bowl, stir together the almond meal, cocoa, coconut flour, baking soda, and salt until well combined.

3. In a medium bowl, whisk together the eggs, honey, coconut oil, and vanilla.

4. Add the wet ingredients to the dry ingredients and stir to mix well.

5. Carefully fold in the raspberries and chocolate chips.

6. Spoon the batter into the donut pan and tap lightly on the counter to remove air bubbles.

7. Bake for 20 to 25 minutes, until firm.

8. Let cool and serve.

CHAPTER THIRTEEN

30 Paleo Lunches

- Gingered Carrot Soup
- Tuscan Tomato Soup
- Butternut Squash Soup
- Cream of Mushroom Soup
- African Sweet Potato Soup
- Spicy Chicken Soup
- Green Bean Salad
- Chicken Fruit Salad with Tangy Mustard Dressing
- Gingered Lemon Broccoli Salad
- Chicken, Pistachio, and Fig Salad
- Chicken Noodle Salad with Thai Dressing
- Broccoli Turkey Slaw
- Stuffed Bell Peppers
- Stuffed Butternut Squash
- Ratatouille

- Pad Thai
- Citrus Poached Salmon
- Shrimp and Peach Tostadas
- Lettuce Wraps with Spicy Chicken
- Vegetable Chicken Stir-Fry
- Chicken Vegetable Wraps
- Curried Chicken "Couscous"
- Chicken Fajitas
- Barbecued Chicken Fingers
- Turkey Burgers with Plum Salsa
- Sesame Turkey Meatballs
- Grilled Lamb Skewers
- Herbed Meatballs
- Flank Steak with Caramelized Onions
- Texas Chili

Gingered Carrot Soup

MAKES 6 SERVINGS

You will be delighted with the vibrant orange hue of this soup as well as the sweet-hot flavor. Carrots are a powerful disease fighter because they are high in beta-carotene and other antioxidants including hydroxycinnamic acids and anthocyanins. The heat of the soup comes from fresh ginger, which has been known for centuries to be a natural health remedy. To create an elegant-looking variation, add a spoonful of snowy vegan yogurt and a sprinkle of chopped fresh chives.

1 teaspoon olive oil
1 small yellow onion, peeled and chopped
2 teaspoons minced garlic
2 stalks celery, diced
12 large carrots, peeled and chopped
1 medium sweet potato, peeled and diced
8 cups low-sodium chicken stock
1 teaspoon grated fresh ginger
1 teaspoon nutmeg
¼ cup maple syrup
Sea salt and cracked black pepper to taste

1. In a large stockpot, heat the oil over medium heat. Add the onion, garlic, and celery and sauté until they become translucent.

2. Add the stock, carrots, sweet potato, ginger, and nutmeg.

3. Bring to a boil and then turn down the heat to low and simmer for 60 minutes, or until the vegetables are tender.

4. Remove from the heat and purée the soup with an immersion blender until smooth.

5. Stir in the maple syrup and season with salt and pepper. Reheat, if needed, and serve hot.

Tuscan Tomato Soup

MAKES 4 SERVINGS

The stars of this soup are fresh, plump tomatoes, which are one of the most commonly consumed foods in the world. Tomatoes are very nutritious and quite high in vitamin B6, niacin, potassium, riboflavin, and folate. Spinach is packed full of vitamin K, vitamin A, manganese, folate, and iron, and is incredibly healthy when combined with the tomatoes in this soup. Make a double batch and freeze it to enjoy when you need a boost of spirit and energy.

12 medium tomatoes, cored and cut in half
2 medium carrots, peeled and thinly sliced
4 celery stalks with greens, chopped
1 large sweet onion, chopped
4 cloves garlic
1 tablespoon olive oil
1 tablespoon balsamic vinegar
6 cups low-sodium chicken stock
2 tablespoons chopped fresh basil
2 teaspoons chopped fresh oregano
1 cup shredded baby spinach
Sea salt and cracked black pepper to taste

1. Preheat oven to 350°F.

2. Place the tomatoes cut-side down in a baking dish and scatter the onion, garlic cloves, celery, and carrots on top. Drizzle with the oil and vinegar.

3. Cover the dish with aluminum foil and bake in the oven until the carrots and celery are tender and tomatoes are fragrant, 50 to 60 minutes.

4. Purée the vegetables with 3 cups of chicken stock with an immersion blender until smooth and then transfer to a medium stockpot. Add the remaining stock, basil, and oregano.

5. Heat the soup until steaming and add the spinach.

6. Season with salt and pepper. Serve hot.

Butternut Squash Soup

MAKES 6 SERVINGS

Butternut squash is a member of the gourd family along with melons, pumpkins, zucchini, and cucumbers. It is actually a fruit, but is often treated as a vegetable in recipes. This soup is simple to make and very elegant in appearance, especially if you top it with fresh herbs or toasted pumpkin seeds.

1 teaspoon olive oil

1 medium yellow onion, peeled and chopped

1 teaspoon minced garlic

8 cups low-sodium chicken stock

6 cups butternut squash cut in ½-inch cubes

1 large sweet potato, peeled and diced

½ teaspoon sea salt

1 teaspoon ground nutmeg

½ teaspoon ground ginger

½ teaspoon ground allspice

¼ cup maple syrup

1. Heat the oil in a medium stockpot set over medium-high heat. Add the onion and garlic and sauté until translucent, about 5 minutes.

2. Add the stock, squash, sweet potato, salt, nutmeg, ginger, and allspice and bring to a boil.

3. Reduce the heat to simmer and cook until vegetables are very tender, about 50 minutes.

4. Remove the soup from the heat and purée with an immersion blender until very smooth.

5. Add the maple syrup, taste, and adjust seasoning if needed. Serve hot.

Cream of Mushroom Soup

Mushrooms have a satisfyingly meaty taste and they are the only vegetable or fruit source of vitamin D. Vitamin D helps with the absorption of calcium and phosphorous as well as providing protection from the common cold. So try this soup during the cold months to stay healthy and fit.

1 tablespoon olive oil
6 cups sliced mushrooms
1 small sweet onion, peeled and chopped
2 teaspoons minced garlic
¼ cup arrowroot starch
2 teaspoons chopped fresh thyme
5 cups low-sodium beef stock
½ cup unsweetened almond milk
½ cup plain vegan yogurt
¼ cup red wine or fresh lemon juice
Sea salt and cracked black pepper to taste

1. Heat the oil in a large skillet over medium heat. Add the onion, garlic, and mushrooms and sauté them until the liquid from the mushrooms has evaporated and the vegetables are soft.

2. Whisk in the arrowroot starch and thyme and cook for a minute.

3. Whisk in the stock slowly and then the almond milk.

4. Simmer until the soup thickens slightly, but do not allow it to boil.

5. Whisk in the yogurt and the wine or lemon juice.

6. Purée half of the soup and then stir it back into the remaining soup. Season with salt and pepper. Serve hot.

African Sweet Potato Soup

This soup is usually made with peanut butter, but since that food is not recommended for the Paleo diet, almond or cashew butter substitutes nicely. The best choice for nut butters is to make your own in a food processor by puréeing raw, soaked nuts until they turn into butter. This can take a long time, but at least your nut butter will be totally free of preservatives, bad fats, and sugar.

1 teaspoon olive oil
1 medium sweet onion, peeled and chopped
1 tablespoon minced garlic
2 tablespoons hot or mild curry paste
1 tablespoon ground cumin
1 teaspoon ground coriander
1 teaspoon ground cinnamon
3 medium sweet potatoes, peeled and diced
2 large carrots, peeled and diced
2 celery stalks, diced
8 cups low-sodium chicken stock
½ cup almond butter
1 red bell pepper, seeded and sliced thin
Juice and zest of 2 limes
Sea salt and cracked black pepper to taste
4 teaspoons chopped cilantro

1. Heat the olive oil in a stockpot over medium-high heat.

2. Add the onion, garlic, curry paste, cumin, coriander, and cinnamon.

3. Sauté until the vegetables are tender and the mixture is aromatic.

4. Add the sweet potatoes, carrots, celery, stock, and almond butter.

5. Cover and bring the soup to a boil.

6. Reduce the heat and simmer until vegetables are tender.

7. Add the bell pepper and simmer for 5 minutes.

8. Stir in the lime juice and zest and season with salt and pepper.

9. Serve hot, garnished with the cilantro.

Spicy Chicken Soup

MAKES 6 SERVINGS

Chicken soup is a balm for the body even without the noodles found in Grandma's recipe. This version has some kick, and the addition of bok choy makes it a bit exotic. You can substitute skinless chicken thighs, which are juicier and more flavorful than chicken breasts, if you like.

1 teaspoon olive oil
1 tablespoon minced garlic
1 tablespoon peeled, grated fresh ginger
¼ teaspoon red pepper flakes
8 cups low-sodium chicken stock
2 boneless, skinless chicken breasts, diced
1 cup coarsely shredded baby bok choy
2 medium carrots, peeled and thinly sliced
2 stalks celery, thinly sliced
½ cup coarsely chopped cilantro
4 scallions, finely sliced diagonally

1. Combine the olive oil, garlic, ginger, and red pepper flakes in a large stockpot over medium heat and cook, stirring, until very aromatic.

2. Add the stock and chicken to the pot and bring to a simmer over medium heat.

3. Reduce the heat and simmer until the chicken is cooked through, about 20 minutes.

4. Remove the chicken from the pot with a slotted spoon and shred it.

5. Increase the heat and bring the soup back to a boil.

6. Add the bok choy, carrots, and celery, reduce the heat, and simmer until the bok choy leaves are vibrant green, 3 to 4 minutes.

7. Remove the pot from the heat, and stir in the shredded chicken and cilantro.

8. Serve hot, garnished with the scallions.

Green Bean Salad

Green bean salads are not often made at home because of the common over-processed ones found in supermarkets and even restaurants. This version is incredibly fresh and colorful, and simply flavored with a squeeze of lemon juice and fresh herbs. To blanch the fresh green beans, cook the beans in boiling water for 2 minutes, remove with a slotted spoon to a bowl of ice water to stop the cooking. Blanching cooks the beans just slightly, and makes the beans a bright green.

3 tablespoons fresh lemon juice

½ cup chopped fresh basil

2 tablespoons chopped sun-dried tomatoes

2 tablespoons olive oil

1 teaspoon minced garlic

Sea salt and cracked black pepper to taste

3 cups fresh green beans, trimmed and cut into 1-inch pieces

3 cups fresh yellow beans, trimmed and cut into 1-inch pieces

2 red bell peppers, seeded and minced

½ cup shredded carrots

½ small red onion, thinly sliced

1. In a small bowl, whisk together the lemon juice, basil, sun-dried tomatoes, olive oil, and garlic. Season with salt and pepper.

2. In a large saucepan, blanch the green beans and yellow beans in lightly salted boiling water for 2 to 3 minutes until just crisp-tender. Drain and rinse with cold water to cool.

3. In a large bowl, toss the cooled beans, red peppers, carrots, and onion. Drizzle with the lemon-basil dressing, and toss gently to coat.

4. Cover and chill before serving.

Chicken Fruit Salad with Tangy Mustard Dressing

Chicken combines very well with many ingredients, such as the celery, apples, and almonds in this dish. Chicken breast is used quite a bit in healthy diets because it is extremely nutritious and simple to prepare. A single 4-ounce portion can provide up to 70 percent of the recommended daily amount of protein. Chicken is also high in vitamin B6, niacin, and selenium, which can help reduce the risk of several cancers.

¼ cup olive oil

¼ cup fresh orange juice

Juice of 1 lime

1 teaspoon fresh lemon juice

1 teaspoon Dijon mustard

1 teaspoon honey

1 tablespoon chopped fresh parsley

Salt and cracked black pepper to taste

4 skinless chicken breasts, poached and shredded

2 red apples, cored and chopped

3 celery stalks, cut into thin strips

1 small yellow bell pepper, cut into strips

2 scallions, thinly sliced

4 cups shredded butter lettuce

⅓ cup sliced toasted almonds

1. In a small bowl, whisk together the olive oil, orange juice, lime juice, lemon juice, mustard, and honey until well combined.

2. Whisk in the parsley and season with salt and pepper.

3. In a large bowl, toss together the chicken, apples, celery, bell pepper, and scallions.

4. Add the orange-mustard dressing to the chicken mixture and toss to combine well.

5. Serve a cup of chicken salad over the shredded lettuce and top with almonds.

Gingered Lemon Broccoli Salad

The dressing used for this salad is lovely with many other types of greens, but absolutely sublime with the combination of ingredients found in this colorful dish. The broccoli soaks up the dressing beautifully and is healthful as well. Broccoli is high in dietary fiber, calcium, vitamin C, potassium, and folic acid, which means it can help reduce high blood pressure as well as decrease the risk of certain cancers.

¼ cup plain vegan yogurt

Juice and zest of 2 lemons

2 teaspoons honey

¼ teaspoon grated fresh ginger

3 small heads broccoli, cut into small florets

1 small red onion, finely chopped

½ cup unsweetened dried cranberries

½ cup roasted pumpkin seeds

1. In a small bowl, whisk together the yogurt, lemon zest, lemon juice, honey, and ginger.

2. In a large bowl, toss together the broccoli, red onion, and cranberries.

3. Add the yogurt-lemon dressing to the broccoli mixture and toss to coat.

4. Cover the salad and chill for at least 4 hours to let the flavors meld.

5. Serve sprinkled with pumpkin seeds.

Chicken, Pistachio, and Fig Salad

MAKES 6 SERVINGS

The flesh of figs is luscious and sweet and packed into smooth, velvety skins. You can purchase figs dried, but it is well worth the effort to find them ripe and fresh. Figs are a good source of potassium, dietary fiber, and calcium while being very low in calories. They are a healthy addition to any nutritious diet.

For the dressing:

¼ cup olive oil

2 tablespoons fresh lemon juice

1 tablespoon whole grain mustard

1 tablespoon honey

Sea salt and cracked black pepper to taste

For the salad:

5 cups arugula

2 cups green beans, trimmed and cut into 1-inch pieces

1 cup grape tomatoes, halved

1 small red onion, thinly sliced

2 large cooked, skinless chicken breasts

½ cup roasted pistachio nuts, coarsely chopped

½ cup shredded vegan cheese

6 ripe figs, quartered

Make the dressing:

In a small bowl, whisk together the olive oil, lemon juice, mustard, and honey, and season with salt and pepper; set aside.

Make the salad:

1. In a large bowl, toss the arugula, green beans, grape tomatoes, and red onion with half of the dressing and arrange on a serving platter.

2. Slice the chicken on the diagonal and arrange over the salad. Top with the pistachios, cheese, and figs.

3. Drizzle the remaining dressing over the salad and serve immediately.

Chicken Noodle Salad with Thai Dressing

MAKES 6 SERVINGS

The noodles in this dish are not the standard wheat-based version, but rather fresh zucchini ribbons created with a peeler or mandoline. Zucchini has a very mild taste that is the perfect foundation for the spicy-sweet Thai dressing. Squash is a mild diuretic and is used to stimulate the intestines. Zucchini is also a great source of beta-carotene.

For the dressing:

½ cup fresh lime juice

1 tablespoon peeled minced fresh ginger

1 tablespoon minced garlic

1 tablespoon honey

1 tablespoon gluten-free tamari sauce

Pinch of red pepper flakes

For the salad:

2 chicken breasts, poached and shredded

4 cups zucchini noodles

1 cup bean sprouts

2 stalks celery, thinly sliced

2 medium carrots, peeled and coarsely grated

1 red bell pepper, seeded and sliced into thin strips

1 bunch cilantro, coarsely chopped

Make the dressing:

1. In a small bowl, whisk together the lime juice, ginger, garlic, honey, tamari, and red pepper flakes until well combined.

Make the salad:

1. In a large bowl, toss the chicken, zucchini noodles, bean sprouts, celery, carrots, bell pepper, and cilantro until well mixed.

2. Pour the dressing over the salad and toss until well combined.

3. Chill and serve.

Broccoli Turkey Slaw

A convenient way to prepare this salad is to use packaged broccoli slaw, but you can also shred or grate your own slaw. This is an absolutely beautiful dish with different colors and textures and a complex flavor profile. Toast the sunflower seeds for about 15 minutes in a medium-hot oven to brown them so the taste of the salad is perfect.

1 pound cooked turkey breast, shredded

1 (12-ounce) package shredded broccoli (broccoli slaw mix)

1½ cups seedless red grapes, halved

1 cup coarsely shredded carrot

⅓ cup balsamic vinegar

2 tablespoons olive oil

2 teaspoons maple syrup

Sea salt and cracked black pepper to taste

¼ cup roasted sunflower seeds

1. In a large bowl, combine all of the ingredients except for the sunflower seeds and toss to combine.

2. Serve immediately or cover and chill for up to 24 hours.

3. Sprinkle with the sunflower seeds just before serving.

Stuffed Bell Peppers

MAKES 6 SERVINGS

This is a true comfort food—filling, homey, and easy to make in a pinch. This variation uses shredded chicken instead of the usual ground beef, which makes it a little lighter. If you want to use ground beef, brown it along with the onions and drain off any excess fat.

Olive oil cooking spray

6 green bell peppers, cored and seeded, tops cut off and reserved

2 cups chopped fresh green beans

2 cups cooked shredded chicken

2 large tomatoes, diced

½ cup shredded vegan cheese

1 small sweet onion, peeled and diced

3 teaspoons minced garlic

1 teaspoon minced fresh oregano

Sea salt and cracked black pepper to taste

1 cup low-sodium chicken stock

1. Preheat oven to 375°F.

2. Grease a 13 × 9-inch baking dish with olive oil spray.

3. Place the green peppers into the baking dish, right-side up.

4. In a large bowl, add the green beans, chicken, tomatoes, cheese, onion, garlic, and oregano, season with salt and pepper, and mix together until well combined.

5. Spoon the filling mixture into the 6 peppers, dividing it evenly, and top each with a cut pepper top.

6. Pour the chicken stock into the baking dish.

7. Cover the dish with aluminum foil and cook for about 45 minutes, until the peppers are soft and the filling is hot.

Stuffed Butternut Squash

This recipe can be doubled easily if you need more than two servings, and the squash can be cooked ahead of time if you are looking for a quick lunch. If you want more filling in the dish, simply scoop out some of the roasted squash to create a bigger cavity. Use that extra cooked squash in smoothies, soup, and tasty side dishes or mash it up with a little maple syrup for breakfast.

1 large butternut squash, halved lengthwise and seeded

1 teaspoon olive oil

2 cups cooked nitrate-free sausage meat, crumbled

½ sweet onion, chopped

2 celery stalks, chopped

1 large carrot, peeled and finely diced

½ cup sliced sun-dried tomatoes

2 teaspoons minced garlic

1 tablespoon tomato paste

1 teaspoon chopped fresh basil

1 teaspoon chopped fresh oregano

1 teaspoon chopped fresh thyme

Sea salt and cracked black pepper to taste

½ cup shredded vegan cheese

1. Preheat oven to 375°F. Line a baking sheet with aluminum foil.

2. Brush the squash halves with olive oil and place cut-side down on the prepared baking sheet.

3. Bake in the oven until the squash is tender but still firm when poked with a fork, about 1 hour.

4. In a large bowl, combine all of the other ingredients except for the cheese and mix well.

5. Turn the cooked squash right-side up and spoon the sausage mixture into them.

6. Place the squash back in the oven and bake for 30 minutes, or until the sausage mixture is hot.

7. Top the squash with the cheese and serve.

Ratatouille

If you love vegetables, this dish is absolutely bursting with them. Butternut squash, peppers, eggplant, tomatoes, and zucchini are all perfectly accented with summer herbs and lots of garlic. Garlic is a commonly used herbal cure for many serious and minor health concerns. It is a pungent member of the onion family and is a natural antibiotic and antioxidant. This means garlic helps fight free radicals in the body and promotes a healthy immune system.

1 small eggplant, peeled and cubed

½ medium butternut squash, peeled and cubed

4 large tomatoes, diced

1 yellow zucchini, chopped

2 medium red bell peppers, seeded and diced

1 medium green bell pepper, seeded and diced

1 small red onion, peeled and diced

1 cup low-sodium chicken stock

1 (6-ounce) can tomato paste

2 green onions, chopped

1 tablespoon minced garlic

2 teaspoons chopped fresh basil

2 teaspoons chopped fresh oregano

2 tablespoons chopped fresh parsley

½ teaspoon chopped fresh thyme

Sea salt and cracked black pepper to taste

½ cup shredded vegan cheese

1. In a large saucepan, combine all ingredients except the cheese. Cover and bring to a boil.

2. Reduce the heat and simmer until it becomes a thick, fragrant stew, approximately 1 hour.

3. Taste, adjust seasoning, and serve topped with the cheese.

Pad Thai

Pad Thai has a reputation as a sodium-, fat-, and calorie-packed dish that is very tasty but not very healthful. This recipe is equally delicious but is extremely nutritious. You can substitute other vegetables if you like, but the carrots and zucchini should still be used as the "noodles" to provide structure and bulk; it takes time to make them, but it is worth it. This dish is incredible the next day, if there is any left.

2 medium zucchini

2 large carrots, peeled

2 tablespoons water

½ head cauliflower, cut into florets

1 cup shredded purple cabbage

1 cup bean sprouts

1 cup snow peas

1 green onion, chopped

2 tablespoons tahini

1 tablespoon almond butter

Juice of 1 lime or lemon

2 tablespoons gluten-free tamari sauce

1 tablespoon honey

1 teaspoon minced garlic

½ teaspoon grated fresh ginger

1. Using a mandoline or vegetable peeler, create "noodles" from the carrots and zucchini.

2. Place the vegetable noodles in a large bowl.

3. In a large skillet, heat the water over high heat and add the cauliflower, cabbage, bean sprouts, snow peas, and green onion. Put a lid on the skillet and steam the vegetables, tossing the skillet until they are tender, 3 to 5 minutes.

4. In a small bowl, whisk together the tahini, almond butter, lime juice, tamari, honey, garlic, and ginger.

5. Pour the tahini-ginger sauce over the vegetables in the skillet and toss to combine.

6. Spoon the sauce and vegetables onto the "noodles" and toss.

7. Let sit for a few minutes to allow the flavors to meld. Serve hot, cold, or at room temperature.

Citrus Poached Salmon

MAKES 4 SERVINGS

You can make this fish recipe the day or evening before to enjoy for a quick lunch the next day. Salmon is valued nutritionally because it is a great source of omega-3 fatty acids, which help reduce the risk of many cardiovascular problems, improve brain health, and decrease inflammation in the joints. Purchase certified wild salmon whenever possible, and keep in mind that there are contamination issues associated with some farmed fish.

8 cups water
⅓ cup fresh lemon juice
1 small yellow onion, sliced
1 clove garlic, crushed
1 large carrot, peeled and thinly sliced
1 cup celery leaves, coarsely chopped
1 tablespoon chopped fresh thyme
1 teaspoon cracked black pepper
1 teaspoon chopped fresh dill
2 bay leaves
½ teaspoon sea salt
4 (8-ounce) salmon fillets

1. Place all the ingredients except the salmon fillets in a large pot and bring to a boil.

2. Immediately reduce the heat to low and gently simmer the liquid for about 1 hour.

3. Remove from the heat and cool the poaching liquid for about 10 minutes.

4. Strain the liquid through a fine sieve or a piece of cheesecloth into a large, wide skillet; discard the solids.

5. Place the skillet over low heat and bring the poaching liquid to a gentle simmer.

6. Carefully add the salmon fillets in one layer.

7. Cover the skillet and simmer the salmon for about 10 minutes, or until it looks opaque and is just cooked through.

8. Remove the salmon fillets carefully from the liquid and let them cool completely.

9. Serve the poached salmon with fresh sliced cucumbers or your favorite salad.

Shrimp and Peach Tostadas

MAKES 4 SERVINGS

This is the perfect dish for a relaxed lunch on a sunny patio with friends, accompanied by a refreshing pitcher of tart lemonade. The tortillas are crisp, the shrimp savory, and the peach salsa is sweet and hot. You can also substitute mango, plums, or papaya for the peaches if you want a different taste sensation.

1 tablespoon olive oil

1 teaspoon minced garlic

½ pound medium shrimp, shelled and deveined

4 Paleo tortillas

Juice of 2 limes

1 ripe peach, pitted and diced

1 small red bell pepper, julienned

½ cup chopped chives

1 jalapeño pepper, seeded and minced

½ teaspoon salt

2 cups shredded romaine lettuce

½ cup plain vegan yogurt

1. Preheat oven to 375°F.

2. Place the olive oil in a large skillet over medium-high heat and sauté the garlic for 1 minute.

3. Add the shrimp to the skillet and sauté until it is pink and opaque, about 2 minutes.

4. Remove the shrimp and place it into a bowl to cool with some ice.

5. Place the tortillas on a baking sheet and bake in the oven for about 10 minutes, turning halfway through, until crisp.

6. Drain the shrimp and discard any ice that is left in the bowl. Add the lime juice, chopped peach, red pepper, chives, jalapeño pepper, and salt to the shrimp and toss to combine.

7. Top the crisp tortillas with the shredded romaine lettuce and then the shrimp mixture.

8. Serve with a small dollop of vegan yogurt.

Lettuce Wraps with Spicy Chicken

The Asian-themed sauce in these fresh lettuce wraps is created with smoky sesame oil, tamari sauce, and almond butter rather than sodium- and preservative-packed prepared sauces. It infuses the chicken with deep flavors that combine perfectly with the milder vegetables and crunchy romaine wrap. You can substitute any vegetable in this pretty lunch, such as bean sprouts and snow peas, for a different delicious variation.

For the sauce:

½ cup almond butter

2 tablespoons water

2 tablespoons fresh lemon juice

2 tablespoons honey

2 teaspoons sesame oil

2 teaspoons arrowroot starch

1 teaspoon minced garlic

1 teaspoon gluten-free tamari sauce

For the wraps:

1 teaspoon olive oil

1 pound skinless, boneless chicken breast, cut into thin strips

1 tablespoon minced fresh ginger

2 teaspoons minced garlic

1 cup sliced button mushrooms

1 cup grated carrots

1 small red bell pepper, cut into thin strips

1 small yellow bell pepper, cut into thin strips

4 scallions, thinly sliced

1 head romaine lettuce leaves, separated

Make the sauce:

1. In a small bowl, whisk the sauce ingredients together until well combined.

2. Taste to adjust the seasoning.

continued ▶

121

30 Paleo Lunches

Make the wraps:

1. Heat the olive oil over medium-high heat in a skillet.

2. Add the chicken breast and sauté until cooked through. Transfer the chicken to a plate.

3. Sauté the ginger and garlic in the skillet for about 30 seconds.

4. Add the mushrooms, carrots, and bell peppers and sauté until they are softened, about 5 minutes.

5. Add the cooked chicken to the skillet and pour in the sauce. Sauté until the sauce has thickened, about 3 minutes.

6. Remove the pan from the heat and toss in the scallions; let cool for 10 minutes.

7. Wrap the warm filling in the lettuce leaves and serve.

Vegetable Chicken Stir-Fry

MAKES 6 SERVINGS

This dish is perfect for a quick lunch because it uses chicken that's already cooked. You can use pretty much any protein with good results, or enjoy it as a vegetarian stir-fry. The jicama in the dish adds a nice crunch and soaks up the sauce beautifully. Jicama, a member of the potato family, is crisp and juicy with a grainy texture. It can be found in most grocery stores and Asian markets.

¼ cup water

3 tablespoons gluten-free tamari sauce

2 tablespoons maple syrup

1 teaspoon peeled grated fresh ginger

1 tablespoon sesame oil

1 head broccoli, cut into small florets

3 stalks celery, sliced

2 small carrots, peeled and cut into thin disks

½ cup sliced jicama strips

½ cup sliced mushrooms

1 large red bell pepper, cut into thin strips

1 small yellow zucchini, cut into disks

½ cup snow peas, trimmed and strings removed

2 cups cubed cooked chicken

½ cup slivered almonds, toasted

1. In a small bowl, mix the water, tamari, maple syrup, and ginger; set aside.

2. Heat the sesame oil in large skillet or wok over medium-high heat.

3. Add the broccoli, celery, carrots, jicama, and mushrooms and sauté for about 5 minutes, stirring constantly.

4. Add the bell pepper, zucchini, and snow peas; stir-fry for 3 minutes, or until the vegetables are softened.

5. Add the chicken and sauté for 2 minutes, until the chicken is warmed through.

6. Add the reserved tamari-ginger sauce and toss to coat.

7. Top with sliced almonds and serve over cauliflower "couscous" (see page 126).

Chicken Vegetable Wraps

MAKES 4 SERVINGS

Eggplant is not usually used in wraps, but it is a very delicious addition in this recipe. Eggplant can soak up fat like a sponge when cooked, so take care not to apply too much oil or dressing directly to the vegetable. Eggplant is high in potassium, niacin, and vitamins A and C. This combination of nutrients is beneficial for conditions such as diabetes and cardiovascular disease.

1 tablespoon olive oil
1 small eggplant, cut into ¼-inch thick slices
2 red bell peppers, cored, seeded, and cut into 1-inch strips
1 yellow bell pepper, cored, seeded, and cut into 1-inch strips
2 medium green zucchini, cut lengthwise into strips
1 small red onion, sliced
Sea salt and cracked black pepper to taste
3 cooked chicken breasts, thinly sliced
2 large tomatoes, cut into slices
8 Paleo tortilla wraps
½ cup Paleo basil pesto

1. Toss the olive oil, eggplant, red and yellow bell peppers, zucchini, and red onion in big bowl and season with salt and pepper.

2. Preheat the barbecue to medium-high heat.

3. Grill the vegetables until they are soft and slightly charred, about 7 or 8 minutes.

4. Remove the vegetables from the barbecue and set aside in a bowl.

5. Spread 1 tablespoon of basil pesto on each wrap and top with some of the sliced chicken, tomato slices, and grilled vegetables. Fold and serve.

Curried Chicken "Couscous"

MAKES 4 SERVINGS

Cauliflower makes an absolutely wonderful substitute for couscous in any recipe. You can grate it by hand, which can get quite messy, or you can pulse it in a food processor until it is the right consistency. Cauliflower is a great source of vitamin C, vitamin K, many B vitamins, and omega-3 fatty acids, which makes it excellent for cardiovascular health, brain function, and digestive health.

1 tablespoon olive oil

1 small red bell pepper, seeded and diced

½ small sweet onion, chopped

1½ cups low-sodium chicken stock

1 head cauliflower, finely grated

½ cup chopped dried apricots

1 teaspoon curry powder

¼ teaspoon sea salt

Pinch of cinnamon

1 cup diced, cooked, skinless chicken breast

2 scallions, thinly sliced

2 tablespoons toasted sliced almonds

1. In a large saucepan heat the olive oil over medium-low heat.

2. Add the bell pepper and onion and sauté for about 2 minutes, or until the onion is translucent.

3. Add the stock to the saucepan and bring to a boil. Remove from the heat.

4. Add the cauliflower, apricots, curry powder, salt, and cinnamon and stir to combine.

5. Cover the saucepan and let steam for approximately 10 minutes.

6. Heat the cooked chicken breast in a microwave for about 30 seconds until it is just warmed.

7. Fluff the cauliflower "couscous" with a fork and add the chicken, scallions, and toasted almonds; toss well. Serve immediately.

Chicken Fajitas

MAKES 4 SERVINGS

This dish is designed for festive eating-with-your-hands, laughter-packed get-togethers. The various elements of the dish can be placed separately in bowls around the table, and Paleo tortillas can also be used for wrapping as well as crisp lettuce leaves. The chicken and bell pepper mixture can be made ahead of time and reheated.

¼ cup olive oil

Juice of 4 lemons

4 tablespoons minced garlic

1 tablespoon chili powder

1 tablespoon ground cumin

1 tablespoon chopped fresh oregano

1 tablespoon ground coriander

2 pounds boneless, skinless chicken breast, cut in thin strips

3 medium sweet onions, peeled and sliced thinly

2 red bell peppers, seeded and sliced into thin strips

2 yellow bell peppers, seeded and sliced into thin strips

4 cups shredded lettuce

2 large tomatoes, cored and diced

2 ripe avocados, peeled, and diced

1. In a large bowl, whisk together the olive oil, lemon juice, garlic, chili powder, cumin, oregano, and coriander until well blended.

2. Add the chicken to the bowl and toss to coat.

3. Place the bowl in the fridge so the chicken can marinate for at least 4 hours.

4. Place a large skillet over medium-high heat and add the chicken and marinade to the heated skillet.

5. Sauté, stirring constantly, until the chicken is cooked through, about 12 minutes.

6. Add the onions and red and yellow bell peppers to the skillet and continue sautéing until the vegetables are softened, about 10 minutes.

7. Serve the chicken on piles of shredded lettuce and topped with tomato and avocado.

Barbecued Chicken Fingers

MAKES 4 SERVINGS

These tasty treats are perfect served with a large fresh salad and a spicy dipping sauce. Let the chicken strips marinate for at least 1 hour to allow the delectable citrus taste to permeate the meat. While the chicken is marinating, if you're using wood barbecue skewers, soak them in water so they don't catch fire over the heat. Simply lay the skewers in a deep container, weigh them down with a can, and cover completely with water.

3 tablespoons olive oil
Juice and zest of 2 large lemons
1½ pounds boneless, skinless chicken breast, sliced into 20 strips
Sea salt and cracked black pepper to taste
20 small wooden skewers, soaked

1. Preheat the barbecue to medium-high heat.

2. In a medium bowl, whisk together the olive oil, lemon juice, and lemon zest.

3. Place the chicken in the marinade and store in the fridge for about 1 hour.

4. Thread each piece of chicken onto a skewer and season with salt and pepper.

5. Grill on the preheated barbecue for about 4 minutes per side, until cooked through. Serve immediately.

Turkey Burgers with Plum Salsa

MAKES 6 SERVINGS

These juicy patties and their tart topping are wonderful served between lightly grilled Portobello mushrooms. Simply grill the mushrooms on the barbecue along with the burgers and set them up like burger buns. You can also use peaches or apricots in the colorful salsa if you can't find ripe plums.

1¾ pounds lean ground turkey

2 ribs celery, minced

½ small red onion, chopped (reserve the other half for the salsa)

1 teaspoon minced garlic

1 teaspoon chopped fresh thyme

½ teaspoon cracked black pepper

Pinch of sea salt

4 plums, pitted and diced

1 small red bell pepper, seeded and chopped

½ red onion, thinly sliced

½ small seedless cucumber, diced

2 tablespoons chopped fresh cilantro

Juice of 1 lime

Cracked black pepper to taste

6 lettuce leaves

1. Preheat barbecue to medium-high heat.

2. In a large bowl, combine the ground turkey, celery, chopped red onion, garlic, thyme, pepper, and salt until well mixed.

3. Shape the turkey mixture into 6 equal-size patties.

4. In a small bowl, stir together the plums, bell pepper, sliced red onion, cucumber, cilantro, lime juice, and pepper. Set the plum salsa aside.

5. Grill the turkey patties for approximately 8 minutes on each side or until cooked completely through.

6. Place each grilled turkey burger on a fresh lettuce leaf and top with plum salsa.

Sesame Turkey Meatballs

Sesame is an unfamiliar flavor for many people who do not experiment with ethnic dishes, but it will become a favorite as soon as you try these tender little meatballs. It is important to toast the sesame seeds to get the full impact on your palate. Simply place the sesame seeds in a small dry skillet and toss them over medium heat until they are light brown and very fragrant.

1 pound ground turkey

2 tablespoons Paleo bread crumbs or almond meal

2 tablespoons toasted sesame seeds

1 large egg, beaten

1 tablespoon gluten-free tamari sauce

2 or 3 scallions, chopped

Sea salt and cracked black pepper to taste

1 tablespoon olive oil

1 cup shredded drained cucumber

6 tablespoons vegan sour cream or plain yogurt

Chopped chives for garnish

6 Paleo tortillas

1. In a large bowl, combine the ground turkey, bread crumbs, toasted sesame seeds, egg, tamari, and scallions.

2. Season with salt and pepper.

3. Mix well and form turkey mixture into meatballs, about 24 total.

4. Heat the oil in a large skillet over medium heat.

5. Cook the meatballs until they are browned on all sides and cooked through, 7 or 8 minutes.

6. Place 4 meatballs on each tortilla and top with shredded cucumber and a spoonful of sour cream.

7. Garnish with chives and wrap.

Grilled Lamb Skewers

Many people do not cook lamb on a regular basis because they think it seems exotic and difficult to spice or handle. But lamb is just as easy to fix as any other meat, and it's so tasty. Lamb is comparable to beef and pork for calories, but since it has less marbling the final cut can be leaner if trimmed. Buy organic lamb to avoid any of the contamination associated with commercially raised animals.

¼ cup fresh lemon juice
2 tablespoons olive oil
2 tablespoons chopped fresh oregano
2 teaspoons minced garlic
Sea salt and cracked black pepper to taste
1 pound lamb leg meat, cut into 1-inch pieces
4 long wooden skewers, soaked in water
1 lemon, cut into quarters

1. In a medium bowl, whisk together the lemon juice, olive oil, oregano, and garlic until well blended, and season with salt and pepper.

2. Add the lamb chunks and toss to coat the meat.

3. Place the bowl in the fridge so the meat can marinate for at least 4 hours.

4. Thread about 5 chunks of marinated lamb onto each skewer.

5. Preheat the barbecue to medium-high.

6. Grill the skewers for about 5 minutes per side, for medium.

7. Serve with lemon wedges.

Herbed Meatballs

MAKES 6 SERVINGS

You can eat these tender meatballs with a nice tossed salad, or you can add them to a plate of fresh vegetable noodles and homemade marinara sauce for a more substantial meal. The combination of pork and beef is very traditional, but you can also create all-beef meatballs if you want a slightly drier variation. Lamb and veal would also be good additions to the mix.

1½ pounds ground pork

½ pound lean ground beef

4 large eggs

1 small sweet onion, peeled and minced

1 cup minced spinach

½ cup minced fresh parsley

½ cup almond meal

¼ cup minced fresh basil

¼ cup minced fresh oregano

1 tablespoon minced garlic

Sea salt and cracked black pepper to taste

1. Preheat oven to 350°F.

2. Cover a baking sheet with aluminum foil.

3. In a large bowl, combine all of the ingredients using your hands until very well mixed.

4. Roll the mixture into golf ball-sized meatballs and place them on the prepared baking sheet.

5. Bake for about 25 to 30 minutes, or until cooked through. Serve hot.

Flank Steak with Caramelized Onions

MAKES 4 SERVINGS

This is a restaurant-quality lunch with complex flavors and a spectacular presentation, so it is a great choice to serve to company. You can wrap these up with lettuce instead of Paleo tortillas if you want a fresher variation. There are some very good Paleo tortilla products to choose from or you can make your own to ensure just the right taste.

1 tablespoon olive oil
2 large sweet yellow onions, thinly sliced
1 red bell pepper, cut into thin strips
1 green bell pepper, cut into thin strips
1 teaspoon minced fresh basil
1 teaspoon minced fresh oregano
1 (1-pound) beef flank steak
Sea salt and cracked black pepper to taste
4 (8-inch) Paleo tortillas, warmed up

1. Heat the olive oil in a large skillet over medium-high heat.

2. Add the sliced onions, reduce the heat to medium-low, cover, and cook until tender, about 10 minutes.

3. Add the bell pepper, basil, and oregano and cook, uncovered, for 4 to 5 minutes. The onions should be golden. Remove from the heat.

4. Trim the fat from the flank steak and season with salt and pepper.

5. Preheat the barbecue to medium-high heat and grill the steak for 8 to 12 minutes, turning once, for medium-rare.

6. To serve, slice the steak thinly, diagonally across the grain.

7. Wrap the steak slices topped with the onion mixture in warm tortillas.

Texas Chili

MAKES 6 SERVINGS

You might have thought your chili days were over on a Paleo eating plan, because what is chili without beans? Many traditional chili recipes, in fact, do not use beans at all, but rather chunks of tender beef infused with savory chili flavor. This recipe adds the richness of sausage for an even more satisfying dish. You can omit the sausage if you are trying to lose weight, but if so, increase the amount of beef.

2 pounds lean ground beef

2 pounds spicy, nitrate-free pork sausage meat

2 large sweet onions, peeled and chopped

2 green bell peppers, seeded and diced

4 teaspoons minced garlic

10 large tomatoes, cored and coarsely chopped

4 tablespoons chili powder, or to taste

2 tablespoons chopped fresh oregano

Sea salt and cracked black pepper to taste

1. Place the ground beef and pork sausage meat in a large pot over medium heat and cook until the meat is browned, stirring constantly.

2. Drain off the excess fat and add the onions, bell peppers, and garlic to the pot.

3. Sauté until the vegetables are soft, 10 to 15 minutes.

4. Add the tomatoes, chili powder, and oregano and reduce the heat to low.

5. Simmer the chili for about 1½ hours, stirring occasionally. Season to taste with salt and pepper. Serve hot.

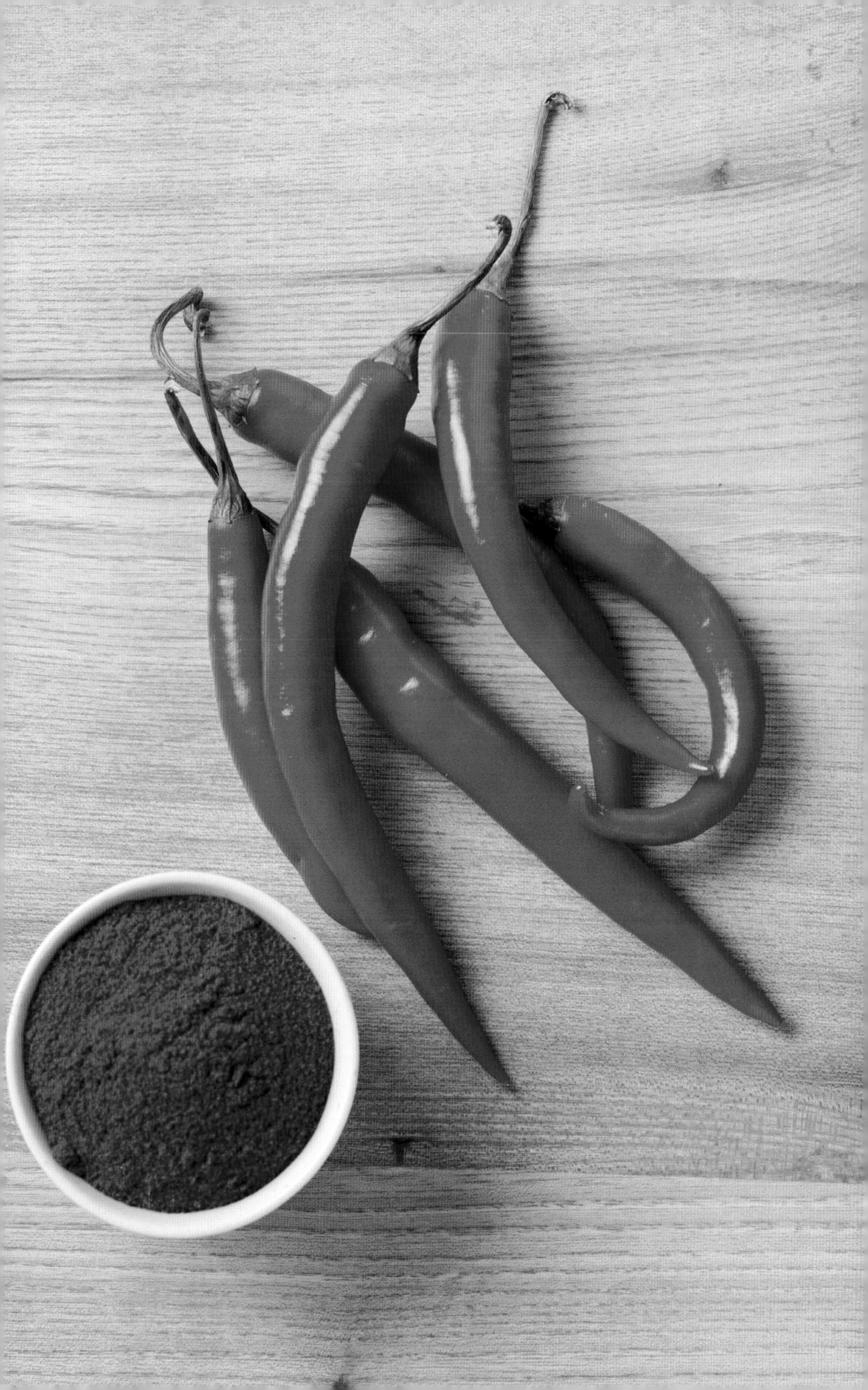

CHAPTER FOURTEEN

30 Paleo Snacks

- Fresh Peach Mango Smoothie
- Sunshine Apple Carrot Smoothie
- Strawberry Spinach Smoothie
- Honeydew Cucumber Smoothie
- Blueberry Almond Smoothie
- Apple Beet Green Smoothie
- Pomegranate Smoothie
- Banana Cantaloupe Smoothie
- Banana Nutella Popsicles
- Strawberry Pineapple Popsicles
- Tender Blueberry Scones
- Chocolate Hazelnut Spread
- Delectable Brownies
- Almond Butter Cups
- Lemon Bars

- Berry Blondies
- Pear Chips
- Maple Roasted Nuts
- Dill Pickles
- Deviled Eggs
- Herbed Beef Jerky
- Sun-Dried Tomato Spread
- Garlicky Red Pepper Dip
- Roasted Eggplant Dip
- Spinach-Artichoke Dip
- Seven Layer Dip
- Crabmeat-Stuffed Mushrooms
- Simple Sweet Potato French Fries
- Buffalo Wings
- Spicy Chicken Wings

Fresh Peach Mango Smoothie

Mango is a luxurious fruit because it is so sweet and so smooth on the tongue. It is the prominent flavor in this pretty, pale yellow smoothie, so you can substitute apricots or plums if peaches aren't ripe enough. Mangos have many health benefits, including lowering cholesterol, promoting healthy skin, and preventing some types of cancers, so make this smoothie a regular weekly snack.

1 cup diced fresh mango
2 ripe peaches, pitted and diced
1 cup unsweetened almond milk
1 cup ice

1. Blend the mango, peaches, and almond milk in a blender and pulse until smooth.

2. Add ice and pulse until well blended.

Paleo for Beginners

Sunshine Apple Carrot Smoothie

This bright, tasty smoothie is almost like carrot cake in a glass. The touch of heat from the ginger and the sweetness of the carrots provide an energizing pick-me-up when you are experiencing a mid-afternoon slump. Make sure your carrots are well cooked so that the smoothie has a silky texture.

2 carrots, peeled and chopped

1 cup applesauce

1 medium apple, peeled, cored, and chopped

½ cup unsweetened almond milk

½ teaspoon peeled grated fresh ginger

1 cup ice

1. Bring 1 water to a boil in a saucepan set over medium-high heat. Add the carrots and cook for about 5 minutes, until the carrots are soft. Drain and cool completely.

2. Combine all of the ingredients in a blender and blend until smooth. Serve immediately.

Strawberry Spinach Smoothie

Spinach and fresh strawberries is delicious in salads, and also works very well in a refreshing smoothie. Strawberries rank fourth among all fruits for antioxidants. It is important to use strawberries right away in drinks like this because studies have shown that the antioxidants and vitamin C can be lost after about 2 days in the refrigerator.

1 pint strawberries, washed and hulled
1 packed cup baby spinach leaves, stems removed
½ cup water
Juice of 2 limes
2 teaspoons grated fresh ginger
1 tablespoon honey
1 cup ice

1. Blend all the ingredients except the ice in a blender until very smooth.

2. Add ice and blend until smooth. Serve immediately.

Honeydew Cucumber Smoothie

This drink is like a blast of energy when you need a quick boost. Both honeydew melon and cucumber are juicy and refreshing, so this is perfect on a hot summer afternoon. Cucumbers are a good source of B vitamins, which help increase energy, and because they are 95 percent water, this beverage is hydrating. Leave the skin on the cukes in this smoothie because it contains a great deal of vitamin C.

2 large English cucumbers with skin, chopped

¼ small honeydew melon, peeled, seeded, and chopped

¼ cup plain vegan yogurt

2 tablespoons chopped fresh mint

1 tablespoon honey

Juice of 1 lemon

1 cup ice

1 lemon, cut into wedges

1. Combine all of the ingredients except the ice in a blender and blend until smooth.

2. Add ice and blend until smooth.

3. Serve immediately, garnished with lemon wedges.

Blueberry Almond Smoothie

Blueberries are considered a super food because they are filled with antioxidants and phytoflavinoids and are very high in vitamin C and potassium. It is their anti-inflammatory properties that really puts them at the top of the nutrition chart. Inflammation in the body can be the key cause of many serious diseases, so reducing inflammation reduces the risks. Blueberries are the perfect, delicious choice for a healthful diet.

1 pint fresh blueberries, picked over
1 small apple, cored and chopped
½ cup unsweetened almond milk
1 tablespoon ground flaxseed
1 tablespoon honey
1 cup ice

1. Combine all of the ingredients except the ice in a blender and blend until smooth.

2. Add the ice and purée until smooth. Serve immediately.

Apple Beet Green Smoothie

Green smoothies have been held up as nutritional essentials in the media for good reason. Dark, leafy greens are packed with nutrients and should be consumed several times a day. This smoothie also has heart-healthy flaxseed, whose major components are omega-3 fatty acids, lignans, and both soluble and insoluble fiber. Studies have linked eating flaxseed to a reduced risk of cancer, diabetes, heart disease, and stroke.

1 small tart apple, cored and chopped
2 packed cups beet greens or spinach
½ cup unsweetened almond milk
½ cup apple juice
1 tablespoon ground flaxseed
1 tablespoon honey
2 cups ice

1. Combine all of the ingredients except the ice in a blender and blend until smooth.

2. Add the ice and blend until smooth. Serve immediately.

Pomegranate Smoothie

MAKES 2 SERVINGS

Pomegranates have a long history as a symbol of health and eternal life in many cultures. The juice can be found year-round in most stores, and fresh pomegranates can be stored in the fridge in sealed bags for as long as two months. If you want to add an extra nutritional punch to this smoothie, top it with a scattering of fresh pomegranate seeds.

½ cup unsweetened almond milk
½ cup unsweetened pomegranate juice
1 large apple, cored, and chopped
1 cup blueberries
1 tablespoon honey
1 cup ice

1. Combine all of the ingredients except the ice in a blender and blend until smooth.

2. Add the ice and blend until smooth. Serve immediately.

Banana Cantaloupe Smoothie

This simple smoothie could easily become a staple because it does not require many ingredients and it is just plain delicious. Drinking it will make you feel full, but still energetic, so it is great for an after-school snack, especially if kids are running out to soccer games or music lessons. Bananas are a fabulous source of potassium, which is essential for a healthy cardiovascular system.

2 ripe bananas, cut into chunks

½ small ripe cantaloupe, peeled and cut into chunks

¼ cup unsweetened almond milk

1 cup ice, or more if you want a thicker smoothie

1. Combine all of the ingredients except the ice in a blender and blend until smooth.

2. Add ice and blend until smooth. Serve immediately.

Banana Nutella Popsicles

MAKES 12 POPSICLES

Many new Paleo enthusiasts are delighted to realize that Nutella is allowed on the diet plan. These popsicles are a perfect way to use Nutella because they taste nearly like Fudgsicles with a hint of hazelnut. Using these treats to introduce kids (and adults) to Paleo is a wonderful way to get them aboard.

7 large ripe bananas

2 cups Nutella or homemade Chocolate Hazelnut Spread (see page 153)

1. Put the bananas in a food processor and pulse until very smooth.

2. Add the Nutella and pulse until smooth.

3. Spoon the mixture into 12 popsicle molds and freeze for at least 6 hours.

Strawberry Pineapple Popsicles

MAKES 8 POPSICLES

You will need to purchase popsicle trays to make these tempting treats. They can usually be found at dollar stores. This recipe calls for the liquid to be poured through a sieve to remove the strawberry seeds, but if you don't mind them you can skip this step. To remove the popsicles from the trays, run hot water briefly over the plastic molds without splashing it on the popsicles. Very simple!

2 cups sliced strawberries
2 cups fresh pineapple juice
¼ cup fresh lime juice
¼ cup maple syrup or to taste

1. Place the strawberries, pineapple juice, lime juice, and maple syrup in a blender and purée until smooth.

2. Pass the liquid through a sieve into a pitcher.

3. Pour the strawberry mixture into popsicle trays and freeze for 4 to 6 hours, or until the popsicles are frozen solid.

Tender Blueberry Scones

MAKES 8 SCONES

Scones call out for rolling hills, dainty tea services, and clotted cream. These beauties can be enjoyed anytime, not just at tea, and can be eaten warm or cold. If you have to use frozen blueberries, you might find the scone itself taking on a distinctly blue shade, but they will still taste lovely.

2 cups fine almond meal

½ cup arrowroot starch, divided, plus more for dusting the work surface

1 tablespoon baking powder

½ teaspoon sea salt

1 large egg

¼ cup coconut oil, melted

2 tablespoons maple syrup

1 cup fresh blueberries

1. Preheat oven to 350°F. Line a baking sheet with parchment paper.

2. In a medium bowl, stir together the almond meal, ¼ cup of the arrowroot starch, the baking powder, and salt.

3. In a small bowl, whisk together the egg, coconut oil, and maple syrup.

4. Add the wet ingredients to the dry ingredients and stir until just mixed.

5. In a small bowl, toss the blueberries with the remaining ¼ cup arrowroot starch and add to the batter, mixing to combine.

6. Gather the batter into a ball and then press it into a flat circle on a clean, arrowroot-dusted work surface. Cut into 8 equal wedges. Place the wedges on the prepared baking sheet.

7. Bake in the preheated oven for 20 to 25 minutes, or until tender and golden brown.

8. Remove from the oven and cool on a wire rack. Serve warm or at room temperature.

Chocolate Hazelnut Spread

MAKES ABOUT 1 ³/₄ CUPS

If you are hesitant about using Nutella when eating Paleo, this recipe is very close to the real spread. You might want to double the recipe because it will vanish quickly. Be patient while processing the ingredients; it may take 10 minutes or more to get the right creamy texture.

2 cups blanched roasted hazelnuts
½ cup full-fat coconut milk
¼ cup pure maple syrup
¼ cup cocoa powder
1 teaspoon pure vanilla extract
Pinch of sea salt

1. Put the hazelnuts in a food processor and process until very smooth, about 10 minutes.

2. Add the coconut milk, maple syrup, cocoa, vanilla, and salt and pulse until the mixture is very creamy and smooth.

3. Transfer the spread to a sealable container and store in the refrigerator.

Delectable Brownies

MAKES 9 TO 12 BROWNIES

Moist, densely chocolaty, and slightly sweet, these brownies are best made a day in advance because they get more intensely flavored the longer they sit. The sweet potato purée is completely undetectable, which means these are perfect lunch stuffers for kids who do not like to eat their vegetables.

Coconut oil for greasing the baking dish

1 cup sweet potato purée

1 ripe avocado, peeled and pitted

½ cup unsweetened applesauce

¼ cup maple syrup

1 teaspoon pure vanilla extract

4 large eggs

½ cup cocoa powder

¼ cup coconut flour

2 tablespoons arrowroot starch

1 teaspoon baking soda

½ teaspoon sea salt

½ cup pecan pieces

1. Preheat oven to 375°F. Lightly grease a 9-inch square baking dish and line it with parchment paper.

2. Place the sweet potato, avocado, applesauce, maple syrup, and vanilla in a food processor and pulse until very smooth and creamy.

3. Add the eggs one at a time and pulse, scraping down the sides of the bowl after each addition.

4. In a large bowl, combine all the remaining ingredients except the pecans and stir to combine well.

5. Add the wet ingredients to the dry ingredients and stir to combine.

6. Add the pecans and stir until incorporated.

7. Spoon the batter into the prepared pan and bake for about 30 minutes, or until a toothpick inserted in the center comes out clean.

8. Cool on a wire rack for about 30 minutes and then transfer to the fridge to cool completely. Cut into squares and serve.

Almond Butter Cups

MAKES 16 CUPS

Anyone who likes peanut butter cups will love these tasty treats. Homemade almond butter is the best choice, but an organic product is fine as long as it contains no sugar. To get the perfect double dark and light layers, make sure the bottom layer is completely chilled before adding the dark chocolate on top. If the topping gets too firm, remelt it.

2 cups dark chocolate, chopped
1 cup almond butter
Pinch of sea salt
½ cup chopped almonds

1. In a medium bowl placed over a pot of gently simmering water, melt the chocolate, stirring constantly.

2. Remove half of the melted chocolate to a container and stir in the almond butter and the salt until smooth.

3. Spoon the almond butter mixture into paper candy cups, filling them about half full. Place them in the fridge until hardened, at least 1 hour.

4. Remelt the plain dark chocolate, if necessary, and spoon it evenly over the chilled almond cups.

5. Place them back in the fridge until completely chilled, about 1 hour.

6. Store the almond cups in the freezer in a sealed container.

Lemon Bars

MAKES 9 SQUARES

These bars taste like lemon meringue pie without the fluffy top. It would also work well with limes, or even oranges or tangerines. If you use oranges, cut the honey down to about 1 tablespoon, depending on the sweetness of your fruit.

For the crust:
Coconut oil to grease baking dish
1 cup coconut flour
1 cup almond flour
3 large eggs
½ cup coconut milk
¼ cup coconut oil
2 tablespoons honey
½ teaspoon cinnamon

For the filling:
8 large eggs
Juice of 6 lemons
1 tablespoon pure vanilla extract
½ cup honey
¾ cup unsweetened shredded coconut

Make the crust:

1. Preheat the oven to 350°F. Lightly grease a 9-inch square baking dish with coconut oil.

2. In a medium bowl, stir together all the crust ingredients until well combined. Press the crust mixture evenly into the prepared pan.

Make the filling:

1. In a medium bowl, whisk together all of the filling ingredients, except the shredded coconut, until blended.

2. Pour the filling mixture over the crust.

3. Bake in the oven for about 30 minutes.

4. Remove from the oven and sprinkle with the shredded coconut.

5. Cool completely on a wire rack and cut into 9 large squares. Serve at room temperature.

Berry Blondies

These look more like rum balls than pale brownies and should be stored in the freezer so they keep their texture. For a truly delicious accent, lightly toast the coconut in a 300-degree oven before rolling the cookies in it. You can also use finely chopped nuts for a coating with no loss of flavor.

6 dates, pitted
1 cup pecans
1 cup roasted cashews
3 tablespoons coconut oil, melted
½ cup diced strawberries
Unsweetened shredded coconut, to coat

1. Line a baking sheet with parchment paper.

2. Place the dates in a food processor and pulse until they form a paste.

3. Add the pecans and cashews and pulse until finely chopped.

4. Add the coconut oil in a thin stream while the processor is running.

5. Transfer the mixture to a bowl and use your hands to carefully mix in the diced strawberries.

6. Roll the mixture into golf ball–sized balls and roll them in the shredded coconut.

7. Store in a container in the freezer until ready to serve.

Pear Chips

Any kind of chip can be made in a dehydrator instead of the oven, if you have one. These finished chips can be either crunchy or chewy, depending on your preference. Simply keep them in the oven until the desired texture is reached, turning them a few times during the process.

6 pears, skin on, cored and cut lengthwise into thin slices
3 tablespoons fresh lemon juice

1. Preheat the oven to the lowest possible temperature and line 2 baking sheets with parchment paper.

2. Transfer the pear slices to the sheets, placing them in a single layer, and lightly brush them with the lemon juice.

3. Place the sheets in the oven with the door propped open and dehydrate for 8 to 10 hours, or until crisp.

4. Remove the chips from the sheets while they are still warm. Let cool.

5. Store the pear chips in a sealed container at room temperature.

Maple Roasted Nuts

MAKES 6 CUPS

Nuts are a perfect portable snack that provides many nutritional benefits. Nuts are a good source of calcium, protein, and healthy fat. You can use an assortment of nuts in this recipe or a single favorite, such as pecans or almonds. These make a nice gift packed into a pretty cookie tin.

Coconut oil to grease the pan
3 egg whites
⅓ cup maple syrup
¼ teaspoon sea salt
Pinch of ground cinnamon
6 cups mixed raw nuts

1. Preheat oven to 375°F. Line a baking sheet with aluminum foil and grease the foil with a bit of coconut oil.

2. Whisk together the egg whites, maple syrup, salt, and cinnamon in a medium bowl.

3. Add the nuts to the egg white mixture and toss them to coat completely.

4. Transfer them to the prepared baking sheet in one layer.

5. Bake for 20 to 25 minutes, stirring a couple of times so they do not burn.

6. When the nuts are golden brown, remove them and let cool to room temperature in the pan.

7. Store in airtight containers at room temperature.

Dill Pickles

These naturally fermented pickles are perfect for the Paleo diet and for anyone else who is looking for a healthier version of this favorite. They are crunchy and perfectly sour, and infused with the taste of dill and garlic. You can eat the garlic or use it in another recipe, as well, because it will be pickled, too.

16 cups small pickling cucumbers, soaked and well scrubbed

2 bunches fresh dill

16 cloves garlic

¼ cup pickling spices

½ cup sea salt, divided

8 cups water

1. Take a large, clean, fermenting jar and layer the cucumbers, dill, garlic, pickling spices, and ¼ cup of the salt into the jar.

2. In a large bowl, whisk together the remaining salt and the water until the salt is completely dissolved to make the brine.

3. Pour the brine into the fermenting jar so that the cucumbers are completely covered.

4. Place the jar, covered, in a warm spot and let the pickles ferment for 5 to 10 days.

5. Keep tasting them until they are the strength you like, and then transfer the jar to the fridge, where they can be stored for several months.

Deviled Eggs

MAKES 24 DEVILED EGGS

Deviled eggs are usually packed with lots of mayonnaise and sodium, so this healthy version is a culinary dream. Eggs are often thought to be unhealthy, but when eaten in moderation they have many benefits. They contain nine amino acids and vitamin D. Studies have shown that eggs can help prevent the formation of cataracts because they contain lutein and zeaxanthin.

12 large hard-boiled eggs, peeled and cut in half
3 tablespoons olive oil
1 small celery stalk, minced
1 teaspoon whole grain mustard
Pinch of smoked paprika
Sea salt and cracked black pepper to taste
4 teaspoons chopped chives for garnish

1. Carefully remove the yolks from the eggs and place them in a small bowl.

2. Add the olive oil, celery, mustard, and paprika and mash until smooth and well combined. Season with salt and pepper.

3. Spoon the yolk mixture back into the egg whites.

4. Top with the chives. Serve immediately or refrigerate until ready to serve.

30 Paleo Snacks

Herbed Beef Jerky

Any kind of jerky is very simple to make at home with either an oven or a dehydrator. The trick to getting great long-lasting jerky that will not spoil is to start with very lean meat completely trimmed of fat. This recipe can also be made using other meats such as buffalo, elk, or venison.

2 teaspoons onion salt

¾ teaspoon cracked black pepper

¾ teaspoon dried oregano

½ teaspoon sea salt

½ teaspoon garlic powder

½ teaspoon dried thyme

½ teaspoon dried basil

2 pounds lean steak, fat trimmed and cut into ¼-inch strips

1. Preheat the oven to the lowest possible temperature. Line two backing sheets with aluminum foil.

2. In a small bowl, mix together all the herbs, spices, salt, and pepper until well blended.

3. Arrange the beef strips on a cutting board and rub half the spice mixture into the meat. Pound the meat with a mallet to work the spice mixture in deeply.

4. Turn all the strips over and repeat the process with the rest of the spice mixture.

5. Transfer the strips to the prepared baking sheets, placing them in a single layer, and put them in the oven with the door propped open.

6. Leave the beef strips in the oven for about 8 hours to dry, and then flip them over and dry them on the other side for 8 hours.

7. Store the jerky in an airtight container at room temperature.

Sun-Dried Tomato Spread

MAKES 3 CUPS

Unless you are a raw food enthusiast or vegan, you might not realize that when raw cashews are soaked and puréed, they become creamy and perfect for sauces and dips. Cashews are actually seeds, not nuts, that are found on the bottom of the cashew apple. You will never find them sold in their shells because the shell contains a resin used to make varnish and insecticide.

2 cups raw cashews, soaked for 8 hours and drained
1 cup sun-dried tomatoes
1 scallion, chopped coarsely
1 tablespoon minced garlic
Juice of 2 lemons
Sea salt and cracked black pepper to taste

1. Place the drained cashews in a food processor and pulse until very smooth and creamy.

2. Add all the remaining ingredients except the salt and pepper.

3. Pulse until smooth and evenly mixed.

4. Season with salt and pepper.

5. Serve with crudités.

Garlicky Red Pepper Dip

MAKES 4 SERVINGS

Roasted red peppers are a favorite ingredient in many recipes because of their rich, distinctive flavor and because they go well with many other ingredients. Many people don't realize that green peppers are just red peppers that have not ripened yet, and that is why the red ones are so much sweeter. Red peppers have substantially more vitamin C than immature green ones. Since vitamin C is essential for iron absorption, it is a great idea to consume red peppers and foods such as spinach together for maximum benefit.

8 medium red bell peppers
1 tablespoon minced garlic
Pinch of sea salt
1 cup shredded vegan cheese
¼ cup fresh lemon juice
1 tablespoon olive oil
¼ cup chopped fresh basil
Cracked black pepper to taste

1. Preheat the oven to broil and cover a baking sheet with aluminum foil.

2. Place the red peppers on the baking sheet and broil in the preheated oven for about 5 minutes per side, or until the skins are charred.

4. Remove the peppers from the oven and place them into a large steel, ceramic, or glass bowl. Cover tightly with plastic wrap and let stand for about 20 minutes to loosen the skins.

5. When the peppers are cool enough to handle, strip the blackened skin off and remove the seeds and stems.

6. Rinse the skinned peppers under cool water and place them in a food processor. Pulse to purée.

7. Add the rest of the ingredients except the basil and pulse to combine.

8. Stir in the chopped basil and season with pepper.

9. Serve with fresh vegetables.

Roasted Eggplant Dip

MAKES 2 CUPS

Eggplant has very little fat in it and acts like a sponge when cooked, so take care when drizzling it with oil. Some studies say that eggplant should not be consumed in large quantities by people with arthritis.

3 small eggplants, peeled and sliced
1 tablespoon sea salt
3 tomatoes, cored and cut into wedges
1 red onion, chopped
3 cloves garlic, lightly crushed
¼ cup olive oil
Juice of 1 large lemon
2 teaspoons chopped fresh parsley, divided
1 teaspoon chopped fresh oregano
¼ cup kalamata olives
1 tablespoon maple syrup

1. Preheat the oven to 350°F.

2. Place the eggplant slices in one layer in a roasting pan and sprinkle with sea salt. Let stand for about 30 minutes to draw the bitterness out of the eggplant.

3. Dry the eggplant with paper towels.

4. Place the eggplant, tomatoes, onion, and garlic in the roasting pan and drizzle with the olive oil and lemon juice.

5. Add 1 teaspoon of the parsley and the oregano.

6. Roast the vegetables in the preheated oven until the eggplant is very tender, about 1 hour.

7. Let the vegetables cool in the roasting pan.

8. Transfer the eggplant mixture, including any accumulated juices, to a food processor and pulse until the mixture is chopped up.

9. Add the olives and maple syrup to the processor and pulse until coarsely chopped.

10. Spoon the dip into a serving bowl and top with the remaining 1 teaspoon of parsley.

11. Chill and serve with crudités or Paleo flatbread.

Spinach-Artichoke Dip

MAKES ABOUT 3 CUPS

Conventional spinach-artichoke dip is full of fat, sodium, and calories because it is often made with mayonnaise. This healthy version tastes the same and can be whipped together as easily. If you want to use frozen spinach instead of fresh, make sure it is a product with no added salt, and squeeze it out well after it is thawed. Too much added water will ruin the texture of the dip.

1 tablespoon olive oil

1 small sweet onion, chopped

2 teaspoons minced garlic

4 cups canned artichoke hearts, drained and chopped

1 teaspoon sea salt

½ teaspoon cracked black pepper

Cayenne pepper to taste

4 packed cups baby spinach, blanched, cooled, well drained, and chopped

1 tablespoon fresh lemon juice

2 cups cashew butter

1. Heat the olive oil in a large skillet over medium heat and sauté the onion and garlic until softened, about 5 minutes.

2. Add the artichoke hearts, salt, pepper, and cayenne and sauté until heated through.

3. Add the chopped spinach and lemon juice to the skillet and stir to combine and heat through.

4. Stir in the cashew butter until the dip is well combined and still warm.

5. Transfer to a serving dish and serve warm with Paleo crackers.

Seven Layer Dip

This dip features multiple layers of spicy beef, creamy avocado, colorful vegetables, olives, and cheese. It is perfect for entertaining or when watching an important sporting event. The dip is loaded with fiber, protein, and many essential nutrients from the vegetables. Try dipping Paleo-friendly bread, crackers, and crudités in it.

1 pound lean ground beef

1 teaspoon chili powder

½ teaspoon ground cumin

½ teaspoon ground coriander

1 large avocado, peeled, pitted, and mashed with the juice of 1 lime

1 cup vegan sour cream or plain yogurt

1 red bell pepper, seeded and chopped

1 green bell pepper, seeded and chopped

1 small red onion, chopped fine

1 cup sliced black olives

5 large tomatoes, coarsely chopped

2 cups shredded vegan cheese

3 sliced scallions for garnish

1. In a small skillet over medium-high heat, brown the beef with the chili powder, cumin, and coriander until cooked through. Drain the beef and spread it on the bottom of a 10-inch shallow serving dish.

2. Spread the avocado over the beef layer.

3. Spread the sour cream over the avocado layer.

4. Next, layer on the bell peppers, onion, olives, tomatoes, and cheese.

7. Garnish with the scallions.

8. Refrigerate for at least 2 hours, until completely chilled.

9. Serve with crudités or oven-baked Paleo tortillas.

Crabmeat-Stuffed Mushrooms

MAKES 4 SERVINGS

These snacks can be prepared ahead of time and popped in the oven when you need them. They are sublime with ½ teaspoon of horseradish mixed into the crab filling if you like a bit of heat. Simply grate a little fresh horseradish very fine instead of getting prepared products. Paleo yogurt and mayonnaise are now being sold at markets like Whole Foods and Costco.

16 large mushrooms
8 ounces fresh crabmeat
¼ cup plain Paleo yogurt or mayonnaise
Juice of half a lemon
1 scallion, just the white part, minced
2 tablespoons minced mushroom stems
Sea salt and cracked black pepper to taste

1. Preheat the oven to 350°F. Line a baking sheet with aluminum foil.

2. Wipe the mushrooms clean and carefully remove the stems.

3. Mince the stems.

4. In a medium bowl, stir together the crabmeat, yogurt, lemon juice, scallion, and minced mushroom stems.

5. Season with salt and pepper.

6. Spoon the crabmeat mixture into the mushroom caps.

7. Place mushroom caps on the prepared baking sheet and bake in the preheated oven for 20 minutes, or until the filling is hot and the mushrooms softened.

8. Remove from the oven and cool slightly on paper towels. Serve warm.

Simple Sweet Potato French Fries

MAKES 4 SERVINGS

These crispy beauties are baked in the oven instead of fried in oil, so they are completely guilt free. Sweet potatoes get sweeter when cooked, so don't add honey or maple syrup to them. They are high in B vitamins, potassium, and magnesium, which means these pretty fries are a wonderful source of energy.

6 sweet potatoes, peeled and cut into 1-inch wedges
4 teaspoons olive oil
Sea salt to taste
Spices such as cinnamon, cumin, or nutmeg

1. Preheat the oven to 350°F. Line a baking sheet with aluminum foil.

2. In a large bowl, toss together the sweet potato wedges, oil, and salt.

3. Spread the potato wedges on the prepared baking sheet and bake for 30 to 45 minutes, until they are crispy on the outside and tender inside.

4. Allow to cool slightly, and then sprinkle with spices, if desired. Serve immediately.

Buffalo Wings

MAKES 6 SERVINGS

The traditional Buffalo wing sauce is a combination of vinegar, butter, and cayenne that originated in Buffalo, New York. This recipe omits the butter and vinegar, but the finished wings still taste similar to the original. Do not skip the steaming step because it adds juiciness to the wings while cutting the cooking time.

24 chicken wings
¾ cup coconut oil, melted
½ cup hot sauce, to your own taste
2 teaspoons minced garlic
½ teaspoon sea salt
Cracked black pepper to taste

1. Fill a large pot with 1 inch of water, place over medium-high heat, and place a steamer basket inside. Bring the water to a boil.

2. Put the wings in the steamer basket, cover, and reduce the heat. Steam the wings for about 15 minutes, then take them out and pat dry.

3. Place the wings on a baking sheet lined with paper towels and cool completely in the fridge.

4. Preheat the oven to 400°F. Line a baking sheet with parchment paper.

5. Place the cooled wings on the parchment paper and bake in the preheated oven for 35 to 40 minutes, turning once, until cooked through and brown.

6. In a large bowl, whisk together the melted coconut oil, hot sauce, to your own taste, garlic, and salt until well blended.

7. When wings are cooked through, transfer them to the bowl and toss until the sauce coats them completely. Serve hot.

Spicy Chicken Wings

MAKES 2 LARGE SERVINGS

These wings should be heaped on a huge platter during any sports event because they are juicy, hot, and snapping with spices. It is well worth the time to toast and grind the spices in this dish—the flavor will be exceptional. You can also use a scrupulously clean coffee grinder for spices. You might find yourself getting a spice grinder just for these addictive wings.

1 tablespoon cumin seeds

1 tablespoon black peppercorns

2 dried red chiles

Juice of 2 lemons

¼ cup olive oil

3 tablespoons honey

3 cloves garlic, crushed

1 tablespoon peeled grated fresh ginger

1 tablespoon tomato paste

Sea salt to taste

16 chicken wings

1. Place the cumin seeds, peppercorns, and chiles in a skillet over medium-hot heat and dry roast them until very fragrant.

2. Transfer them to a food processor or use a mortar and pestle to grind them very finely.

3. In a large bowl, combine the ground spice mixture, lemon juice, olive oil, honey, garlic, ginger, and tomato paste and whisk to combine. Season with salt.

4. Add the chicken wings to the bowl and toss to coat with the marinade. Place the bowl in the fridge for 2 to 4 hours to let the flavors meld.

5. Preheat the oven to 375°F. Line a baking sheet with aluminum foil.

6. Arrange the chicken wings on the prepared baking sheet, shaking off the excess marinade, and bake for about 45 minutes, turning once, until cooked through. Serve immediately.

CHAPTER FIFTEEN

30 Paleo Dinners

- Mediterranean Fish Stew
- Sole Florentine
- Grilled Halibut with Pepper Salsa
- Tomato Baked Halibut
- Blackened Tilapia
- Baked Salmon with Roasted Beets and Greens
- Cajun Spiced Salmon
- Roasted Salmon with Fennel
- Chili Lime Shrimp
- Shrimp Paella
- Scallops with Grilled Pineapple Salsa
- Lemon Chicken
- Chicken Cacciatore
- Almond-Crusted Chicken
- Chicken Shepherd's Pie
- Chicken Meatloaf

- Moroccan Chicken
- Slow-Cooked Chicken Korma
- Lamb Tagine
- Pork and Apple Casserole
- Pork Chops with Spiced Apples and Thyme
- Savory Beef Stew
- Grainy Mustard-Crusted Pork Tenderloin
- Home-Style Meatloaf
- Spicy Pasta Puttanesca with Meat Sauce
- Beef Stroganoff
- Beef Short Ribs
- Osso Buco
- Beef Chow Mein
- Venison with Mustard and Herbs

Mediterranean Fish Stew

Deep bowls of spicy vegetable- and fish-packed stews are common in countries that border oceans and seas. This version would not be out of place in France, Italy, or Spain, where the tomatoes burst with color and flavor. You can substitute any combination of fish in this dish, depending on what is fresh at your local market. When it comes to fish-based cuisine, freshness is the key rather than precisely following the recipe.

1 tablespoon olive oil

1 large sweet onion, diced

2 teaspoons minced garlic

1 hot chile pepper, seeded and finely chopped

4 large tomatoes, chopped

3 tablespoons tomato paste

1 cup dry white wine

1 cup low-sodium fish stock

Zest of 1 orange

4 skinless halibut fillets, cut into chunks

1½ pounds shrimp, peeled and deveined

1 pound fresh clams, in the shell

1 cup shredded spinach

¼ cup chopped fresh parsley

1 tablespoon chopped fresh thyme

Sea salt and cracked black pepper to taste

1. Heat the olive oil in a large pot over medium-high heat. Add the onion and sauté until it becomes translucent, about 5 minutes.

2. Add the garlic and chile pepper to the pot and sauté until softened, about 2 minutes.

3. Add the tomatoes and tomato paste and bring the mixture to a boil. Reduce the heat and simmer for about 10 minutes.

4. Add the white wine and simmer until most of the liquid is evaporated, 5 to 10 minutes.

5. Add the fish stock and orange zest and stir to combine well.

6. Carefully add the halibut chunks and simmer for 5 to 7 minutes. Add the shrimp and clams and simmer 5 to 7 more minutes, until all or most of the clams have opened.

7. Remove and discard any unopened clams. Stir in the spinach, parsley, and thyme. Season with salt and pepper. Serve hot.

Sole Florentine

This recipe is a healthier version of a classic dish. Sole is a mild, delicate fish that cooks quickly. It is very low in fat and high in protein, selenium, iodine, and B vitamins. Sole can contribute to an effective cardiovascular system and thyroid health. If you cannot find fresh sole, you can use frozen sole in this recipe with very little loss of texture. To blanch the spinach, use same technique for blanching green beans on page 107.

1 tablespoon olive oil
1 small onion, chopped
½ teaspoon minced garlic
2 packed cups spinach, blanched, squeezed out, and chopped
Sea salt and cracked black pepper to taste
2 pounds fresh sole
Juice of 1 lemon
½ cup grated vegan cheese
1 teaspoon minced fresh dill
Lemon wedges for garnish

1. Preheat a large skillet over medium-high heat and add the olive oil.

2. Sauté the onion and garlic until softened, about 5 minutes.

3. Add the spinach to the skillet and stir to combine.

4. Remove from the heat and season with salt and pepper.

5. Place the sole on the spinach mixture and squeeze the lemon juice over it.

6. Sprinkle the cheese evenly over the fish.

7. Cover the skillet and reduce the heat to medium.

8. Cook for 10 to 15 minutes, or until the sole flakes easily and is cooked through.

9. Serve hot, topped with dill and lemon wedges.

Grilled Halibut with Pepper Salsa

MAKES 4 SERVINGS

You can use any firm-fleshed fish in this recipe with great results because the salsa really steals the show. Grilled or roasted peppers have a rich, smoky flavor that is perfect with mild-tasting fish and even chicken. For the best texture, be sure to follow the instructions for steaming the charred skins off of the peppers.

1 tablespoon plus 1 teaspoon olive oil, divided
1 small green zucchini, trimmed and cut lengthwise into strips
½ small red onion, peeled and cut into thick disks
2 red bell peppers
1 yellow bell pepper
1 tablespoon balsamic vinegar
10 fresh basil leaves, torn
1 teaspoon minced garlic
Juice of 1 lime
4 (6-ounce) halibut fillets
Sea salt and cracked black pepper to taste

1. Preheat the barbecue to medium-high heat.

2. In a medium bowl, toss 1 teaspoon of the olive oil with the zucchini and red onion.

3. Place the red and yellow bell peppers on the grill and char on all sides. Grill the zucchini and red onion alongside.

4. Place the charred bell peppers in a small bowl and cover tightly with plastic wrap for about 10 minutes; steam will loosen the skin.

5. Peel, seed, and dice the skinned bell peppers and put them in a small bowl.

6. Chop the grilled zucchini and red onion coarsely and add them to the bell peppers.

7. Add the vinegar, basil, garlic, and lime juice to the bell pepper salsa.

8. Brush the fish fillets on both sides with the remaining 1 tablespoon of olive oil.

9. Season the fish on both sides with salt and pepper.

10. Grill the fish until it is opaque, about 3 minutes per side or until it flakes easily with a fork.

11. Spoon the bell pepper salsa on top of the fish and serve.

Tomato Baked Halibut

MAKES 4 SERVINGS

Casserole-style dishes are great when you are trying to feed a family or need left-overs for the next day's lunch. This double tomato sauce is even more delicious the second day, so it is a perfect choice for people with limited kitchen time. Sun-dried tomatoes are very easy to create yourself in large batches in the oven. Simply cut small plum tomatoes or cherry tomatoes in half, toss in a little olive oil and sea salt, then spread them in a single layer on a baking sheet and pop it in an oven set to the lowest temperature. Prop the door open and let the tomatoes slowly dry overnight.

Olive oil spray
1 tablespoon olive oil
1 small sweet onion, sliced
1 teaspoon minced garlic
10 plum tomatoes, chopped, with juice reserved
½ cup chopped sun-dried tomatoes
Sea salt and cracked black pepper to taste
4 (6-ounce) halibut steaks
2 tablespoons chopped fresh basil

1. Preheat the oven to 400°F. Grease a 9 × 13-inch baking dish with olive oil spray, and set aside.

2. Heat a skillet over medium heat and add the olive oil.

3. Add the onion and garlic to the skillet and sauté, stirring, until they just begin to brown, about 5 minutes.

4. Stir in the plum tomatoes and their juice and the sun-dried tomatoes.

5. Season with salt and pepper.

6. Sauté for about 5 minutes; remove from heat.

7. Place the fish fillets in the prepared baking dish in a single layer.

8. Spoon the tomato mixture over the fish.

9. Bake for 10 to 15 minutes, or until the fish flakes easily.

10. Remove from the oven and serve sprinkled with the basil.

Blackened Tilapia

Tilapia has recently gained popularity because it will not break most budgets and its mild taste is the perfect base for many different flavors. Tilapia is low in fat and high in protein, which is superb for vibrant health. Tilapia is a good choice for meals a couple of times a month, but should not be used frequently because most tilapia is farmed. There are some health concerns associated with farmed fish, so make sure you source yours from a reputable organic provider.

2 tablespoons smoked paprika

1 tablespoon onion powder

1½ teaspoons cayenne pepper

1½ teaspoons dried oregano

½ teaspoon dried thyme

½ teaspoon celery seeds

1½ teaspoons sea salt

½ teaspoon cracked black pepper

¼ teaspoon garlic powder

1½ pounds tilapia fillets

2 tablespoons olive oil

1 lemon, cut into wedges

1. Combine the spices, herbs, salt, and pepper in a medium, shallow bowl and mix well.

2. Dredge the tilapia fillets in the spice mixture, put on a plate, and refrigerate, covered, for about 1 hour to let the flavors meld.

3. Place a large skillet on medium-high heat and add the olive oil.

4. Cook the tilapia in the hot skillet for about 4 minutes per side, blackening the surface of the fish.

5. Serve the fish hot with lemon wedges on the side.

Baked Salmon with Roasted Beets and Greens

MAKES 4 SERVINGS

When preparing this dish, wear gloves, or you will end up with stains from peeling the beets. All that mess will be worth it when you taste the finished result, though, because roasted beets are sublime. If you do get stained, rub your hands in fresh lemon juice and salt until the patches are gone. This solution should only be used if your hands are nick free.

8 medium beets, peeled and cut in cubes

2 cups spinach

4 (6-ounce) salmon fillets

Sea salt and cracked black pepper to taste

4 teaspoons olive oil

4 teaspoons chopped fresh thyme

1. Preheat oven to 450°F.

2. Tear off four 24-inch pieces of 18-inch-wide heavy-duty aluminum foil. Fold each piece in half to make four 18 × 12-inch pieces.

3. Divide the beet chunks evenly among the four pieces of foil, putting them in the center.

4. Top each package of beets with ½ cup of the spinach.

5. Place one piece of salmon on top of each vegetable pile and season with salt and pepper.

6. Top each fillet with a drizzle of olive oil and chopped thyme.

7. Fold the foil to create sealed packages that have a bit of space for steam to collect.

6. Place the salmon packets in a single layer on a baking pan.

7. Bake in the preheated oven for 15 to 20 minutes, checking carefully to make sure the fish does not overcook. It is done when the fish flakes easily with a fork and the beets are tender. Serve immediately, opening the packets carefully to avoid the hot steam.

Cajun Spiced Salmon

MAKES 4 SERVINGS

Cajun spice rub blackens when heated in a pan. To ensure the fiery taste penetrates the fish well, let the rubbed fillets sit in the refrigerator before cooking them. Cajun cuisine is often thought to have originated in Louisiana, but it actually has its roots among the French-speaking Acadians, who emigrated from the northeastern coast of Canada to settle in the southern United States. This spice mix is not overly hot, so if you want more heat, simply add a little cayenne pepper.

2 tablespoons smoked paprika
1 tablespoon ground cumin
1 tablespoon garlic powder
1 tablespoon ground coriander
2 teaspoons cracked black pepper
2 teaspoons minced fresh thyme
1 teaspoon minced fresh oregano
2 pounds salmon fillets
Sea salt to taste
2 tablespoons olive oil

1. In a medium bowl, whisk together all the spices and herbs until well mixed.

2. Pat the salmon fillets dry and lightly season with salt.

3. Place the salmon fillets into the spice mix, coating both sides, put on a plate, and refrigerate, covered with plastic wrap, for 30 to 60 minutes.

4. Place a heavy skillet over medium-high heat and add the olive oil to the pan.

5. When the pan is very hot, sear the salmon fillets for about 4 minutes per side, or until the flesh is just cooked through. Serve immediately.

Roasted Salmon with Fennel

Many people are unfamiliar with fennel as an ingredient, but the licorice-like scent will definitely spark a memory. Fennel looks kind of like celery that has grown out of control. It is bulbous with delicate fronds of pale green in a profusion at the top. These fronds can be saved and used for garnish. Fennel is a great source of vitamin C, folate, and fiber, which means it is extremely heart-friendly. When purchasing fennel, look for pale green to whitish vegetables with no spots, splits, or bruises.

3 fennel bulbs, trimmed, cored, and cut into ½-inch wedges

2 small sweet onions, cut into ½-inch slices

10 cloves garlic

2 large tomatoes, cut into chunks

6 sprigs fresh thyme

2 tablespoons olive oil

6 (6-ounce) salmon fillets

Sea salt and cracked black pepper to taste

Juice and zest of 1 lemon

1. Preheat oven to 400°F.

2. In a large roasting dish, evenly distribute the fennel, onions, garlic, tomatoes, and thyme sprigs.

3. Drizzle with the olive oil and roast in the oven for about 25 minutes.

4. Take the pan out of the oven and use a spatula to flip the vegetables over. Top the vegetables with the salmon fillets in one layer.

5. Season with salt and pepper.

6. Sprinkle the fish with the lemon juice and zest and bake for about 15 minutes, or until the salmon is just cooked. Serve immediately.

Chili Lime Shrimp

MAKES 2 SERVINGS

Shrimp on the barbecue is the epitome of summer indulgences, and these tasty morsels are very easy to prepare on nights you need to eat and run. The lime used to flavor the shrimp is a nice change from the usual lemon, and limes offer great health benefits just like their citrus cousins. Limes have much more vitamin C than lemons; they were commonly used on ships to prevent scurvy, which resulted in the nickname "limeys" for English sailors. Limes promote healthy gums, teeth, and bones, as well. Serve the grilled shrimp with a large tossed salad.

1 tablespoon olive oil
Juice and zest of 2 limes
2 tablespoons honey
½ teaspoon paprika
¼ teaspoon chili powder
Cracked black pepper to taste
12 large shrimp, peeled and deveined
4 wood skewers, soaked in water

1. In a medium bowl, combine the oil, lime zest and juice, honey, paprika, chili powder, and pepper.

2. Add the shrimp and toss to coat. Put the bowl in the refrigerator, and let the shrimp marinate for 20 to 30 minutes.

3. Preheat the barbecue to medium-high.

4. Put 3 shrimp on each wooden skewer and barbecue, turning once, until the shrimp are just cooked through, 2 to 3 minutes per side.

5. Serve immediately.

Shrimp Paella

Paella is a classic Spanish dish that is usually rice based. This version substitutes cauliflower for the rice, but retains the traditional flavoring of saffron. Tiny quantities of real saffron are expensive, but the flavor is worth it. Look for saffron from Iran or Spain to be sure the quality is high.

½ pound spicy, nitrate-free sausage meat, removed from casings

1 pound shrimp, peeled and deveined

1 small onion, chopped

1 tablespoon minced garlic

1 teaspoon red pepper flakes

3 medium carrots, peeled and cut into disks

2 red bell peppers, seeded and diced

1 head cauliflower, pulsed in a food processor to resemble rice

1 cup fresh green beans, halved

½ cup low-sodium chicken stock

1 teaspoon chopped fresh thyme

¼ teaspoon saffron threads

Sea salt and cracked black pepper to taste

1. Place a large skillet over medium-high heat and cook the sausage meat until cooked through, not breaking it up too much. Remove the meat with a slotted spoon to a paper towel–lined plate.

2. Add the shrimp to the skillet and sauté until pink and just cooked through, about 2 minutes. Remove to the same plate as the sausage meat.

3. Add the onion, garlic, and red pepper flakes to the skillet and sauté until the onion is translucent, about 5 minutes.

4. Add the carrots and bell peppers to the skillet and stir to combine. Cover the skillet and cook for 5 to 7 minutes, or until the carrots are softened.

5. Add the cauliflower, beans, chicken stock, thyme, and saffron to the skillet and stir to combine.

6. Sauté until the flavors are well mixed and the cauliflower is softened, about 5 minutes.

7. Season with salt and pepper, and stir the shrimp and sausage back into the paella. Serve hot.

Scallops with Grilled Pineapple Salsa

Pineapple is not usually thought of as something to grill, but it is exceptional barbecued. The sugar in the fruit caramelizes and a hint of smokiness makes it seem sweeter. Pineapple isn't just delicious, it is also a wonderful source of dietary fiber, vitamin A, and many antioxidants. This means it can help promote a strong immune system.

½ ripe pineapple, cut into thick disks
2 scallions, sliced thinly on the diagonal
1 small red bell pepper, seeded and diced
1 tablespoon peeled grated fresh ginger
1 tablespoon chopped fresh cilantro
Juice and zest of 1 lime
⅛ teaspoon red pepper flakes
Sea salt and cracked black pepper to taste
8 large scallops, cleaned
2 tablespoons olive oil

1. Preheat the barbecue to medium-high heat.

2. Grill pineapple slices until they are sticky and cooked almost through.

3. Remove from the heat and set aside to cool.

4. When the pineapple is cool, dice it and transfer to a medium bowl.

5. Add the scallions, bell pepper, ginger, cilantro, lime juice, lime zest, and red pepper flakes.

6. Season with salt and pepper and toss to combine well; set aside.

7. Lightly season the scallops with salt and pepper.

8. Heat a large skillet over medium-high heat and add the olive oil.

9. Sear the scallops for about 2 minutes per side until browned, opaque, and just cooked through.

10. Serve hot with the pineapple salsa.

Lemon Chicken

MAKES 4 SERVINGS

If you need a sophisticated dish for company, this recipe will fit your expectations perfectly. Tender chicken slices and vibrant, slightly crisp vegetables are bathed in a balanced citrus- and ginger-infused sauce. This dish also features tamari sauce, which some people confuse with soy sauce. Tamari sauce is similar to soy sauce, but it has little or no wheat in it while also having more flavor and less sodium.

Olive oil cooking spray
2 skinless, boneless chicken breasts, thinly sliced
1 small sweet onion, thinly sliced
1 red bell pepper, seeded and cut into thin strips
1 tablespoon grated fresh ginger
1 teaspoon minced garlic
2 carrots, thinly sliced into discs
1½ cups low-sodium chicken stock
2 tablespoons white wine
3 tablespoons arrowroot starch
2 tablespoons gluten-free tamari sauce
1 tablespoon honey
Juice and zest of 2 lemons
1 teaspoon toasted sesame oil
1½ cups green beans, cut into 2-inch pieces
1 cup bean sprouts

1. Grease a large skillet with olive oil spray and heat over medium-high heat.

2. Add the chicken and sauté until it is just cooked through, about 5 minutes. Remove the chicken with a slotted spoon to a plate.

3. Reduce the heat to medium and add the onion, bell pepper, ginger, and garlic; cook, stirring often, for 5 to 6 minutes.

4. Add the sliced carrots and sauté for 2 minutes.

5. Add the chicken stock and white wine and heat until the liquid is simmering.

6. Cover the pan and simmer for 10 minutes, stirring occasionally.

7. In a small bowl, whisk together the arrowroot, tamari, and honey to make a smooth paste.

8. Whisk in the lemon juice, lemon zest, and sesame oil.

9. Stir the tamari-lemon mixture into the stock in the skillet and bring the liquid to a boil, stirring constantly until thickened.

10. Add the cut green beans and sauté for 2 minutes.

11. Add the bean sprouts and sauté for 2 minutes.

12. Add the chicken back in the skillet and cook another 2 minutes or so, until it is heated through. Serve immediately.

Chicken Cacciatore

MAKES 4 SERVINGS

This dish is actually a very simple stew that seems much more glamorous because of the fancy name. Cacciatore pairs chicken with ripe tomatoes for a satisfying rich taste. This stew definitely promotes good health, with ingredients like tomatoes, celery, carrots, lean chicken, and fresh herbs. These combine to create a meal that is an excellent source of protein and antioxidant power to fight free radicals and promote cardiovascular health.

⅓ cup arrowroot starch

¼ teaspoon sea salt

⅛ teaspoon cracked black pepper

8 chicken thighs, skinned

1 tablespoon olive oil

4 stalks celery, sliced

3 medium carrots, peeled and cut into chunks

1 medium sweet onion, coarsely chopped

4 teaspoons minced garlic

1 cup low-sodium chicken stock

1 cup dry red wine

12 plum tomatoes, diced

¼ cup tomato paste

2 tablespoons chopped fresh thyme

2 tablespoons chopped fresh basil

¼ cup shredded vegan cheese

2 tablespoons chopped fresh flat-leaf parsley

1. In a small bowl, combine the arrowroot, salt, and pepper. Dredge the chicken pieces with this mixture, turning to coat them evenly and shaking off the excess.

2. In a large skillet, heat the oil over medium-high heat.

3. Add the chicken pieces and cook, turning once, for about 4 minutes per side, until the pieces are browned on each side. Remove the chicken from the skillet to a plate.

4. Drain off excess fat and add the celery, carrots, onion, and garlic. Sauté, stirring occasionally, until the onion is tender.

continued ▶

5. Stir in the stock, wine, tomatoes, and tomato paste; bring to a boil.

6. Return the chicken to the skillet and reduce the heat.

7. Simmer, covered, for 60 to 70 minutes, or until the chicken is tender. Stir in the thyme and basil at the very end of cooking.

8. Serve sprinkled with the cheese and parsley.

Almond-Crusted Chicken

MAKES 6 SERVINGS

Nut-crusted chicken breasts are a staple dish in many fine restaurants because the combination tastes and looks decadent. The chicken in this dish is coated in almonds but could easily be dressed in cashews or pecans if you wish. Almonds are a great choice, though, because they have a delicate flavor that does not overwhelm the protein.

Olive oil spray

6 skinless, boneless chicken breasts

2 tablespoons almond butter

1 tablespoon olive oil

1 tablespoon fresh lemon juice

2 teaspoons chopped fresh thyme

1 teaspoon minced garlic

Sea salt and cracked black pepper to taste

½ cup slivered almonds

1. Preheat the oven to 375°F. Cover a baking sheet with aluminum foil and spray it lightly with olive oil spray.

2. Place each chicken breast between two sheets of plastic wrap and pound flat.

3. In a small bowl, stir together the almond butter, olive oil, lemon juice, thyme, and garlic until well mixed.

4. Transfer the pounded chicken breasts to the baking sheet, and season with salt and pepper.

5. Spread the almond butter mixture over the meat.

6. Top the chicken with slivered almonds and bake in the preheated oven for 25 to 30 minutes, or until cooked through. Serve hot.

Chicken Shepherd's Pie

Traditional shepherd's pie usually features ground beef and mashed potatoes, so this tasty sweet potato–topped chicken variation makes a nice variation. The trick to a truly successful shepherd's pie is to completely cook the meat portion of the dish. Top this savory mixture with the mashed sweet potatoes and reheat in the oven until the top is lightly browned and bubbling.

3 large sweet potatoes, peeled and cut into chunks
½ teaspoon olive oil
1 small onion, chopped
2 cups button mushrooms, cut in quarters
2 teaspoons minced garlic
2 cups low-sodium chicken stock
3 tablespoons water
2 tablespoons arrowroot starch
3 poached chicken breasts cut into medium chunks
2 carrots, peeled and cut into thin disks and blanched until tender
2 cups fresh peas
2 teaspoon minced fresh thyme
Sea salt and cracked black pepper to taste

1. Preheat oven to 350°F.

2. Boil the sweet potatoes until very soft; drain and mash, then set aside.

3. Heat the oil in a large skillet, and sauté the onion, mushrooms, and garlic until softened, about 5 minutes.

4. Add the stock to the skillet and heat to a simmer over medium heat.

5. In a small bowl, whisk the water and arrowroot together until there are no lumps.

6. Pour the arrowroot mixture into simmering stock mixture. Stir until the sauce is thick.

7. Add the chicken, carrots, peas, and thyme to the skillet and stir to combine. Season with salt and pepper.

8. Spoon the chicken mixture into a large baking dish and spread the mashed sweet potatoes over the top, completely covering the chicken mixture.

9. Bake until the filling bubbles along the edges, about 35 minutes.

Chicken Meatloaf

MAKES 4 SERVINGS

This healthy version of a traditional, unpretentious dish uses chicken and grated carrots instead of ground beef. Carrots are a common ingredient in many recipes because they provide bulk, are inexpensive, and taste wonderful. Carrots are an important source of beta-carotene, a powerful disease fighter. They are also well known for promoting good vision and supporting a healthy heart.

1 pound lean ground chicken

1 large egg

1 cup white mushrooms, finely chopped

1 large carrot, peeled and grated

½ small onion, chopped fine

½ small red bell pepper, seeded and finely chopped

¼ cup chopped fresh chives

1 teaspoon peeled grated fresh ginger

1 teaspoon minced garlic

Sea salt and cracked black pepper to taste

1. Preheat the oven to 350°F. Line a 4 × 8-inch loaf pan with parchment paper.

2. In large bowl, mix all the ingredients until well combined.

3. Transfer the meatloaf mixture to the prepared loaf pan and pack it down well.

4. Bake for 50 to 60 minutes, or until the meatloaf is cooked through.

5. Remove the meatloaf from the oven and let stand for about 10 minutes.

6. Tip the pan and drain off any visible grease. Slice and serve.

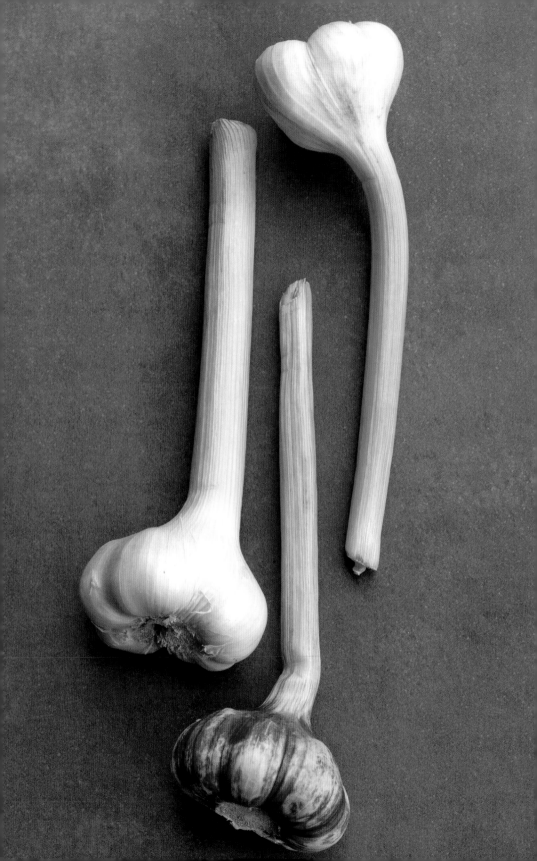

Moroccan Chicken

MAKES 4 SERVINGS

This is a simple recipe that creates strong, distinct flavors. The most time-consuming part of the preparation, besides the marinating time, is cutting up the whole chicken. If you are not confident in your chicken-cutting skills, there are usually cut-up birds in the grocery meat sections, or you can ask your butcher to cut the chicken up for you. The different cuts of the chicken will cook at slightly different times, so make sure you check each piece for doneness.

½ cup fresh lemon juice
1 cup chopped fresh cilantro
1 cup chopped fresh parsley
1 tablespoon minced garlic
1 whole roasting chicken, cut into parts
Sea salt and cracked black pepper to taste

1. In a large bowl, stir together the lemon juice, cilantro, parsley, and garlic until very well mixed.

2. Add the chicken pieces and toss to coat.

3. Place the bowl in the fridge for at least 4 hours to marinate, turning once.

4. Preheat oven to 350°F.

5. Shake the chicken pieces lightly to remove excess marinade and place them in a large baking dish in one layer.

6. Lightly season with salt and pepper and turn the pieces skin-side down in the dish.

7. Cover the dish with aluminum foil and bake in the preheated oven for 1 hour, turning the chicken once.

8. Remove the dish and flip the chicken over to skin-side up. Bake uncovered for an additional 30 minutes, or until the skin is golden and crispy. Serve immediately.

Slow-Cooked Chicken Korma

MAKES 6 SERVINGS

The slow cooker is an invaluable kitchen tool for any household. You can put an assortment of raw ingredients in it in the morning and when you get home there is a delicious hot meal! This tender, spicy dish will welcome you home with the scent of warm spices and garlic. You can easily adjust the heat in this curry by using either hot or mild curry paste or powder. Serve with slices of crisp, cool cucumber and creamy vegan yogurt.

3 cups chicken breast, cubed

3 large sweet potatoes, peeled and diced

6 large tomatoes, diced

1 large sweet onion, coarsely chopped

1 tablespoon minced garlic

1 tablespoon curry paste, mild or hot

½ teaspoon ground cumin

¼ teaspoon ground cloves

¼ teaspoon ground cinnamon

¼ teaspoon sea salt

½ cup plain vegan yogurt

1. Place all of the ingredients except the yogurt into a slow cooker, and stir to combine.

2. Cover and set the temperature on high heat and cook for 3 to 4 hours or on low heat and cook for 6 to 8 hours.

3. Remove the slow-cooker insert from heating element, stir in the yogurt, and serve over cauliflower "couscous" (see page 126)

Lamb Tagine

MAKES 6 SERVINGS

A tagine is a Moroccan earthenware covered vessel used to cook rich stews, also called tagines. You don't need to have this particular vessel to make this recipe; a covered pot will do nicely. Tagines often feature meats, fruits, and spices rather than vegetables. In this case, fresh, plump dates are used. If you cannot find dates, then ripe apricots are also fine, if you add a little honey to provide the sweetness found in dates.

4 tablespoons olive oil, divided
3 pounds lamb shoulder, cut into 8 pieces
2 small onions, finely chopped
1 teaspoon saffron threads (see page 190)
½ teaspoon ground ginger
4 cups low-sodium chicken or lamb stock
1 teaspoon ground cinnamon
Sea salt and cracked black pepper to taste
2 cups dates, pitted
½ cup sliced almonds

1. Heat 3 tablespoons of the olive oil in a large lidded pot over medium heat. Add the lamb and cook, turning, until it is browned on all sides, about 5 minutes. Remove the lamb with tongs and set aside on a plate.

2. Add the remaining 1 tablespoon olive oil to the pot and sauté the onions until they are lightly caramelized, about 7 minutes.

3. Return the lamb and any accumulated juices on the plate to the pot along with the saffron and ginger.

4. Add the stock and bring to a boil. Reduce the heat, cover, and simmer for about 1 hour, stirring occasionally.

5. Add the cinnamon and season with salt and pepper.

6. Simmer uncovered until the sauce is thickened, about 15 minutes.

7. Add the dates and simmer an additional 10 minutes.

8. Serve hot, topped with sliced almonds.

Pork and Apple Casserole

MAKES 4 SERVINGS

This casserole is prepared and cooked in one skillet, so you don't lose a drop of delicious juices. Pork and apples are combined in many recipes because they complement each other perfectly. Use a slightly sweeter, milder apple here. Keep the skin on when dicing them, because this part of the fruit is full of fiber and nutrients. Wash the apples thoroughly even if they are organic to remove any contaminants.

3 teaspoons olive oil, divided
1½ pounds pork tenderloin, cut into chunks
1 small sweet onion, chopped
1 teaspoon minced garlic
2 cups halved mushrooms
2 large carrots, peeled and diced
1 sweet potato, peeled and diced
2 cups full-fat coconut milk
2 apples with skin, cored and diced
2 teaspoons minced fresh thyme
½ teaspoon ground cinnamon
Sea salt and cracked black pepper to taste

1. Preheat oven to 350°F.

2. Place a large skillet over medium-high heat and add 1 teaspoon of the olive oil.

3. Add the pork and cook, stirring frequently, until the meat is browned and just cooked through, 8 to 10 minutes. Remove the pork to a plate.

4. Add the remaining 2 teaspoons of oil and reduce the heat to medium.

5. Sauté the onions and garlic until fragrant and softened, about 5 minutes.

6. Add the mushrooms, carrots, and sweet potato and cook for 10 minutes, or until the vegetables are tender.

7. Add the coconut milk, apples, thyme, and cinnamon, salt and pepper, and the pork to the skillet and stir to combine.

8. Cover the skillet with aluminum foil and bake in the preheated oven for about 30 minutes, until bubbling. Serve hot.

Pork Chops with Spiced Apples and Thyme

Have you ever wondered whether the saying, "an apple a day keeps the doctor away," is true? Well, there is truth in this old folk remedy. Apples are one of the healthiest foods available, especially if organic. They are a great source of soluble fiber called pectin, which makes apples very effective at controlling blood sugar, reducing the risk of many cancers, and lowering cholesterol. This recipe is best with tart varieties of apples to accent the thyme and cinnamon.

1 teaspoon olive oil
4 boneless pork chops, fat trimmed
1 small sweet onion, thinly sliced
2 large tart apples with their skin, cored and sliced thinly
½ cup apple juice
1 tablespoon whole grain Dijon mustard
1 teaspoon chopped fresh thyme
½ teaspoon ground cinnamon
Sea salt and cracked black pepper to taste

1. Preheat oven to 350°F.

2. Heat the olive oil in a large ovenproof skillet over medium heat. Add the pork chops and brown on both sides. Remove the pork chops from the skillet and set aside on a plate.

3. Add the onion to the skillet and sauté until softened, about 5 minutes.

4. Add the apple slices to the onions and sauté until the apples are softened, about 5 minutes.

5. Stir in the apple juice, mustard, thyme, and cinnamon.

6. Move the onion mixture to the side of the pan and return the pork chops to the pan along with any juices on the plate.

7. Spoon the onion mixture over the pork chops, cover, and place the skillet in the preheated oven. Cook until the pork chops are tender, about 35 minutes.

9. Season with salt and pepper, and serve hot.

Savory Beef Stew

This is a wonderful dish for a chilly autumn or winter evening that can be made in double batches and frozen. Don't be tempted to splurge on better cuts of beef for this recipe because the leaner cuts become fork-tender when cooked for a long time. Look for the large cuts that say chuck (roast or shoulder) or bottom (round roast or eye roast), as well as with top round and pot roast.

1 tablespoon olive oil

1 pound lean beef stew meat, trimmed of fat, cut into ½-inch pieces

Sea salt and cracked black pepper to taste

1 large sweet onion, chopped

2 cups halved button mushrooms

4 cups low-sodium beef stock

6 large tomatoes, diced

2 cups diced peeled sweet potatoes

2 large carrots, peeled and diced

1 cup water

2 cups green beans, trimmed and halved

4 cups chopped fresh spinach

½ teaspoon red pepper flakes

1. In a large heavy pot, heat the oil over medium-high heat.

2. Season the stew meat with salt and pepper and brown it in two batches until browned on all sides, about 5 minutes per batch.

3. Remove the stew meat from the pan with a slotted spoon and put on a plate.

4. Add the onion and mushrooms to the pot and sauté for about 5 minutes or until tender.

5. Return the meat to the pot and add the stock, tomatoes, potatoes, carrots, and water.

6. Simmer over medium heat, stirring occasionally, for about 45 minutes or until the meat and vegetables are tender.

7. Stir in the green beans and simmer, covered, for about 15 minutes.

8. Add the spinach and red pepper flakes.

9. Simmer for about 2 minutes, or just until the spinach is wilted. Serve hot.

Grainy Mustard-Crusted Pork Tenderloin

MAKES 4 SERVINGS

When purchasing the mustard for this mouth-watering dish, take a minute to read the label to make sure there are no unwholesome ingredients like sugar or preservatives. Some mustard brands are not as pure as is needed on a Paleo diet. You can also make your own mustard if you really want to know what is in it. You just need mustard seeds, vinegar, white wine, spices, and maybe some chopped shallot.

2 pounds pork tenderloin
Sea salt and cracked black pepper to taste
¼ cup whole grain Dijon mustard
2 tablespoons chopped fresh thyme
2 teaspoons minced garlic

1. Preheat oven to 375°F. Line a baking sheet with aluminum foil.

2. Lightly season the pork tenderloin with salt and pepper and place on the baking sheet.

3. In a small bowl, mix together the mustard, thyme, and garlic.

4. Spread the mustard mixture on the pork, covering the top and sides.

5. Roast in the preheated oven for about 30 minutes, or until just cooked through.

6. Allow to rest for 10 minutes, slice, and serve.

Home-Style Meatloaf

What is more comforting than a thick slab of homemade meatloaf? When you are craving a meal that sticks to your ribs, get the loaf pans out and whip together a few of these hearty creations. The combination of pork and beef makes this meatloaf juicy and less dense than a completely beef-based recipe.

1 onion, finely diced
1 pound ground pork
1 pound lean ground beef
1 cup almond meal
2 large eggs
¼ cup tomato paste
1 tablespoon minced fresh basil
2 teaspoons minced garlic
1 teaspoon chopped fresh thyme
Sea salt and cracked black pepper to taste

1. Preheat oven to 350°F.

2. In a large bowl, combine all of the ingredients until very well mixed. Mix with clean hands.

3. Transfer the meatloaf mixture to a loaf pan and shape into a loaf.

4. Bake in the oven for about 1 hour, or until the middle is no longer pink.

5. Remove from the oven, and let sit for 10 minutes. Remove the meatloaf to a plate, and slice. Serve hot.

30 Paleo Dinners

Spicy Pasta Puttanesca with Meat Sauce

MAKES 4 SERVINGS

This classic pasta sauce has a pleasing salty-spicy taste that pairs well with lean ground beef or even sausage. The saltiness in the sauce comes from the black olives, which are not only delicious, but also very high in iron, vitamin A, vitamin E, and antioxidants. Olives are very good for cardiovascular health as well as cancer prevention, which is why olive oil is considered to be part of any healthy diet plan.

1 pound lean ground beef
1 small onion, chopped
1 tablespoon minced garlic
2 celery stalks, chopped fine
10 large tomatoes, chopped
1 tablespoon chopped fresh basil
1 teaspoon chopped fresh oregano
½ teaspoon red pepper flakes
Sea salt and cracked black pepper to taste
½ cup kalamata olives, pitted and quartered
⅓ cup low-sodium beef stock
Juice of 2 lemons
8 cups zucchini noodles (see page 112)

1. Heat a large pot over medium-high heat. Add the beef and cook, stirring, until browned, about 8 minutes.

2. Add the onion, garlic, and celery and sauté until the vegetables are softened, about 5 minutes.

3. Stir in the chopped tomatoes, basil, oregano, and red pepper flakes.

4. Bring the sauce to a boil, stirring constantly, then reduce the heat and simmer for 20 to 25 minutes.

5. Add the olives, beef stock, and lemon juice, stirring to combine.

6. Spoon the sauce over zucchini noodles and serve.

Beef Stroganoff

MAKES 6 SERVINGS

Imagine tender strips of beef; a fragrant, rich sauce; and lightly caramelized mushrooms all garnished with chopped fresh parsley. Parsley may be thought of as a garnish, but it is actually healthy in its own right. Some studies have shown that parsley could be beneficial for helping with diabetes because it can improve blood glucose levels. Make a generous double batch of this dish and freeze it for future meals. Just leave out the yogurt until it is thawed and reheated, to avoid curdling. The carrot noodles can be made by using a vegetable peeler to shave the carrots into thin strips.

1 teaspoon olive oil

1 pound sirloin, trimmed and cut into thin strips

3 cups sliced white mushrooms

1 small sweet onion, chopped

2 tablespoons minced garlic

1 cup low-sodium beef stock

⅓ cup red wine

2 tablespoons arrowroot starch

½ cup vegan sour cream or plain yogurt

2 tablespoons chopped fresh parsley

Sea salt and cracked black pepper to taste

Carrot noodles

1. Heat the olive oil in a large pan over medium-high heat. Add the sirloin strips and cook until browned, about 3 minutes. Remove the strips with a slotted spoon and set aside on a plate.

2. Add the mushrooms, onion, and garlic to the pan and sauté until golden, about 5 minutes.

3. Whisk in the beef stock, red wine, and arrowroot until well combined.

4. Return the beef to the pan and stir until the beef is tender and the sauce is thick and glossy.

5. Add the sour cream and parsley, and season with salt and pepper; mix to combine.

6. Serve over the carrot noodles.

Beef Short Ribs

This recipe takes some planning and time to prepare well, so it is a good choice for lazy weekends or holidays. Short ribs are tender and meaty when cooked very slowly so the meat falls off the bone. You can either buy ribs in one thick slab and cut them yourself or get them precut. Make sure you get the thicker side of the rack of ribs rather than the tapered side so there is more meat.

12 beef short ribs
Sea salt and cracked black pepper to taste
2 tablespoons olive oil
8 celery stalks, chopped
4 carrots, peeled and cut into 1-inch chunks
2 small onions, chopped
1 fennel bulb, diced
2 tablespoons minced garlic
8 cups dry red wine
¼ cup tomato paste
8 cups low-sodium beef stock
6 sprigs fresh thyme
6 sprigs fresh rosemary

1. Preheat oven to 400°F. Cover two baking sheets with aluminum foil and place the short ribs on the sheets.

2. Season the meat lightly with salt and pepper.

3. Roast in the oven for about 20 minutes. Remove from the oven and lower the temperature to 300°F.

4. Place a large roasting pan on the stove on medium heat and add the olive oil.

5. Sauté the celery, carrots, onions, and fennel until the vegetables have softened, about 15 minutes.

6. Add the garlic and sauté for 3 minutes.

7. Add the red wine and tomato paste to the pan and bring to a boil. Boil until the liquid is reduced by half.

8. Add the short ribs to the pan along with the beef stock and herb sprigs.

9. Cover and place the pan in the oven for about 2 hours, until the meat is falling off the bone.

10. Take the pan out of the oven and carefully remove the meat to a plate.

11. Remove the herb sprigs and discard, and bring the liquid back to a boil on the stove.

12. Simmer until the sauce is reduced by about half, about 15 minutes.

13. Put the meat back into the sauce and serve.

Osso Buco

This delectable meal scares away home cooks because they feel it must be incredibly complicated to prepare. Osso buco means "bone with a hole" in Italian, and it is actually a peasant dish that is a simple braise. The most difficult part of this preparation will be searching the finished dish to find the fresh herb sprigs and cloves so you can discard them. If you want to eliminate that hassle, simply tie them up in a piece of cheesecloth and remove the whole bundle before serving.

6 meaty veal shanks, about ¾ pound each

2 tablespoons olive oil

3 celery stalks, diced

3 small carrots, peeled and diced

2 small sweet onions, diced

2 teaspoons minced garlic

2 tablespoons tomato paste

2 cups dry white wine

5 cups low-sodium chicken stock

3 sprigs fresh thyme

2 sprigs fresh rosemary

2 bay leaves

4 whole cloves

¼ cup chopped fresh parsley

Zest of 1 lemon

1. Pat the veal shanks dry and set them on a plate. Tie butcher's twine around the outside of the shanks to keep the meat from falling off the bone during cooking if you wish.

2. Place a large skillet over medium-high heat and add the olive oil.

3. Brown the shanks for about 4 minutes per side and set them on the plate.

4. Add the celery, carrots, onions, and garlic to the skillet and sauté until the vegetables are softened, about 5 minutes.

5. Stir in the tomato paste and put the veal shanks back in the pan.

6. Add the white wine and boil until the wine is reduced by half, about 5 minutes.

continued ▶

7. Add the chicken stock, thyme, rosemary, bay leaves, and cloves and bring the liquid back to a boil.

8. Reduce the heat to medium-low, cover, and simmer for about 90 minutes. The liquid in the skillet should cover the veal by about three-quarters, so add more liquid if required.

9. When the shanks are tender, remove the pan from the heat and remove and discard the herb sprigs, bay leaves, and cloves from the cooking liquid.

10. Serve hot, garnished with chopped parsley and lemon zest.

Beef Chow Mein

MAKES 4 SERVINGS

Beef is the cornerstone of the Paleo diet for many people, so it is important to know how to pick the best product. When choosing beef, look for a uniform, clear color that is not too bright. Make sure the beef has a good marbling of fat, which adds flavor and tenderness to the meat, and will ensure a flavorful dish.

2 teaspoons sesame oil
1 pound beef strip loin steak, sliced
4 stalks celery, trimmed and sliced
3 large carrots, peeled and sliced into thin disks
2 cups sliced button mushrooms
4 scallions, chopped
1½ cups low-sodium beef stock
½ cup gluten-free tamari sauce
2 tablespoons honey
1 teaspoon peeled, grated fresh ginger
Red pepper flakes to taste
1 cup snow peas, trimmed
1 cup bean sprouts
1 red bell pepper, seeded and julienned
⅓ cup arrowroot starch
⅓ cup water

1. Heat the oil in a very large skillet or wok on medium-high heat.

2. Add the beef slices and cook until just a little pink; remove with a slotted spoon onto a plate.

3. Stir-fry the celery, carrots, mushrooms, and scallions until the vegetables are crisp-tender, about 5 minutes.

4. Add the stock, tamari, honey, ginger, and season with red pepper flakes; continue to cook, stirring, for 2 minutes.

5. Add the snow peas, bean sprouts, and bell pepper and stir-fry for 3 minutes.

6. In a small bowl, whisk the arrowroot and water until very smooth.

7. Stir the arrowroot mixture into the skillet. Cook until sauce is thickened and shiny.

8. Return the beef to the pan and cook, stirring, until the beef is hot.
Serve immediately.

CHAPTER SIXTEEN

30 Paleo Desserts

- Fresh Gingered Cantaloupe
- Poached Pears
- Spiced Pear and Applesauce
- Barbecued Peaches with Cinnamon
- Toffee Apples
- Ambrosia with Coconut and Almonds
- Slow-Cooked Peach and Plum Confit
- Vanilla Custard
- Vanilla Bean Cream with Peaches
- Mango Almond Custard
- Slow-Cooked Carrot Pudding
- Decadent Chocolate Mousse
- Chocolate Fondue
- Dark Chocolate Pots de Crème
- Lime Cookies

- Lemon Slices
- Coconut Snowballs
- Cantaloupe Granita
- Coconut Sorbet
- Pineapple Gelato
- Strawberry Ice Cream
- Apple Crumble
- Pecan Pie
- Rich Chocolate-Banana Pie
- Apple Pie Cupcakes with Spiced Frosting
- Coffee Streusel Cake
- Creamy Cheesecake
- Chocolate Snack Cake
- Molten Chocolate Lava Cake
- Chocolate Mug Cake

Fresh Gingered Cantaloupe

Fresh fruit with a hint of spice can be a great dessert for a meal of fish or a light chicken salad. Use a ripe cantaloupe for the best flavor. Cantaloupe is a delicious source of many nutrients such as vitamin C, fiber, folate, vitamin A, vitamin B3, and vitamin B6, which contribute to a healthy immune system and good vision.

2 small ripe cantaloupes, peeled and cubed
¼ cup honey
2 tablespoons peeled grated fresh ginger

1. Place the cantaloupe in large serving bowl.

2. Add the honey and toss to combine well.

3. Grate the ginger over the cantaloupe. Taste as you go until you have achieved the desired heat.

4. Discard the ginger pulp and toss the cantaloupe to distribute the flavors.

5. Transfer to serving bowls and serve immediately.

Poached Pears

When you are served these elegant, tender pears in a fancy restaurant, it is impossible to imagine how easy they are to make at home. Classic poached pear recipes usually include wine and sugar, so this very healthy version highlights the fruit more than the sauce. You can certainly add a couple of tablespoons of honey to your poaching liquid for a sweeter pear, but it really isn't necessary if the fruit is nice and ripe. You can core the pears with a melon baller or an apple corer.

1½ cups apple juice
1 teaspoon ground cinnamon
1 teaspoon ground nutmeg
4 whole pears, carefully peeled, cored from the bottom, stems left attached
½ cup sliced strawberries

1. In a small bowl, whisk the apple juice, cinnamon, and nutmeg together.

2. Place the pears in a shallow saucepan.

3. Add the juice mixture to the pears and set the pan over medium heat.

4. Bring the liquid to a simmer but do not boil. Reduce the heat to low and simmer for about 30 minutes, turning the pears frequently, until tender.

5. Transfer the pears carefully to a serving plate.

6. Garnish with the strawberries and serve immediately.

30 Paleo Desserts

Spiced Pear and Applesauce

MAKES 6 SERVINGS

This dessert is not fancy, but it can be exactly the right note to end a casual family meal. Pears add a hint of grainy texture to the dish that is pleasing. The skin is kept on the pears because studies have shown the it contains more phenolic phyto-nutrients than the flesh, as well as half the fruit's fiber. Since the skin can also be a source of contaminants, wash pears thoroughly before eating.

8 tart apples, peeled, cored, and sliced
4 pears, cored and sliced
1 cup apple juice
½ cup maple syrup
½ teaspoon ground cinnamon
½ teaspoon ground nutmeg

1. Place all of the ingredients in a saucepan set over medium-high heat and bring to a simmer.

2. Reduce the heat to low and simmer for about 1 hour, or until apples and pears are tender.

3. Mash coarsely with a potato masher and serve warm or cold.

Barbecued Peaches with Cinnamon

MAKES 4 SERVINGS

It is impossible to imagine how delicious peaches are when grilled if you have not tried them. The sugars in ripe peaches caramelize and don't require any extra sweetener. Try this with homemade Paleo vanilla or coconut ice cream for a decadent dessert.

6 ripe peaches, halved and pitted
3 tablespoons coconut oil, melted
½ teaspoon ground cinnamon

1. Preheat the barbecue to medium-low heat.

2. Brush the coconut oil to cover the peach halves completely.

3. Place the peaches on the hot barbecue and grill for about 3 minutes per side, until soft and beginning to brown.

4. Sprinkle a little ground cinnamon on the cut sides of the peaches and serve them while still hot.

Toffee Apples

These sticky, juicy treats will bring out the kid in anyone. Timing is crucial when making and chilling the caramel, because if it is too thick you will not be able to roll the apples in it. Make sure your apples are completely dry before applying the caramel or it will simply slip right off the fruit. If you cannot get the caramel to coat the apples evenly and neatly, don't despair; it also works as a delectable dip with crisp apple wedges.

2 cups raw cashews

¾ cup maple syrup

½ cup plus 2 tablespoons water

3 tablespoons coconut oil

1 tablespoon pure vanilla extract

Pinch of sea salt

8 firm tart apples, washed and stems removed

8 wooden candy apple sticks

1½ cups finely chopped nuts, optional

1. Place the cashews, maple syrup, water, coconut oil, and vanilla in a blender and process until very smooth. This is the caramel mixture.

2. Transfer the caramel to a deep medium bowl and place it in the fridge, covered, until the caramel is thick, 15 to 20 minutes.

3. Place the chopped nuts in another bowl.

4. For each apple, insert a wood stick three-quarters of the way through the bottom.

5. Dry the washed apples thoroughly with a paper towel.

6. Carefully dip the apples in the caramel so that they are completely covered, and then roll them in the nuts, if desired.

7. Place the finished apples on a plate and chill them standing up in the fridge until firm. Serve cold.

Ambrosia with Coconut and Almonds

Ambrosia is a traditional Southern dish that features fruit, coconut, and marsh-mallows. This version omits the marshmallows but still maintains its "food of the gods" reputation. The fruit can be changed with the season, although pineapple combines perfectly with the coconut.

1 cup slivered almonds, toasted in the oven for 10 minutes

1 cup unsweetened flaked coconut, toasted in the oven until lightly browned

1 cup plain vegan yogurt

2 tablespoons honey

½ teaspoon ground cinnamon

1 small ripe pineapple, peeled, cored, and cubed

5 oranges, segmented

3 ripe peaches, pitted and sliced into thin wedges

2 bananas, sliced

1. In a small bowl, combine the toasted almonds and coconut.

2. In another small bowl, whisk together the yogurt, honey, and cinnamon.

3. In a large bowl, mix all the fruit together until well combined.

4. Divide the fruit among 6 dessert bowls. Spoon the yogurt over the fruit and sprinkle evenly with the toasted almonds and coconut.

5. Serve immediately.

Slow-Cooked Peach and Plum Confit

MAKES 6 SERVINGS

This recipe is like an applesauce made with stone fruit, so expect a nice sauce-like texture when the fruit softens. Plums are exceptionally healthful and contain unique phytonutrients called neochlorogenic and chlorogenic acid, which are extremely effective for neutralizing free radicals in the body. Plums are also a great source of vitamin C, they help with iron absorption, and they reduce the risk of atherosclerosis.

8 ripe peaches, pits removed

12 ripe plums, pits removed

½ cup apple juice

½ cup maple syrup or honey

1 teaspoon cinnamon

½ teaspoon ground ginger

Zest of 1 lemon

1. Place all ingredients in a slow cooker and stir to combine.

2. Cover the pot and cook on low heat for 6 to 7 hours.

3. Serve hot or cold, or freeze to enjoy later.

Vanilla Custard

MAKES 6 SERVINGS

Vanilla is a favorite flavor in many cultures, and this creamy custard is infused beautifully with real vanilla bean. Vanilla beans have small amounts of vitamin B and traces of iron, potassium, and calcium. This combination can help regulate the metabolism, normalize heart rate, and promote healthy red blood cells.

2 cups unsweetened almond milk
1 vanilla bean, split
⅓ cup honey
5 large eggs
½ teaspoon ground cinnamon

1. Preheat the oven to 325°F.

2. In a small saucepan set over medium-high heat, cook the almond milk, split vanilla bean, and honey until the mixture just reaches a boil. Remove from heat and remove the vanilla bean. Scrape the seeds from the bean into the scalded milk. Rinse and save for another use.

3. In a large bowl, whisk the eggs.

4. Add the warm almond milk mixture to the eggs, whisking constantly, until well blended.

5. Pour the custard through a fine-mesh sieve into a pitcher.

6. Pour the custard into 6 ramekins.

7. Place the ramekins in a baking dish and pour very hot water into the dish, taking care not to splash any water in the custard, until the water comes about 1 inch up the sides of the ramekins.

8. Carefully place the pan into the oven and bake until the custard is set but not overcooked, 35 to 40 minutes.

9. Remove from the oven and chill in the fridge until set and cold.

Vanilla Bean Cream with Peaches

MAKES 6–8 SERVINGS

Peaches and cream is a classic combination that can still be enjoyed when you are not consuming dairy products. This pudding is pale, smooth, creamy, and sweet. If your blender is not powerful, chop the nuts and coconut as fine as possible so you won't have to process them forever to get the right texture. This dish would also be delicious with any kind of ripe fruit, so experiment to find your favorite combination. You can scrape out the seeds from the vanilla bean, and keep the bean for another use.

6 cups chopped young coconut meat

1 cup raw cashews, soaked for 8 hours in water and drained

20 dates, pitted

1 cup coconut water or coconut milk

1 vanilla bean, split, and seeds scraped out

1 teaspoon pure vanilla extract

3 cups sliced ripe peaches

1. Place all of the ingredients except the peaches in a food processer and blend until very smooth and thick.

2. Transfer to a serving bowl and chill completely in the refrigerator.

3. Serve the purée chilled and drizzled over the sliced peaches.

Mango Almond Custard

MAKES 6 SERVINGS

This creamy, fruity treat, lightly sweetened with honey, is basically a crème brûlée without the crispy sugar topping. It would be easy to add some crushed maple sugar to the top and caramelize it with a cook's propane torch for a elegant end to a meal.

2 cups unsweetened almond milk
¼ cup honey
5 eggs
1 tablespoon pure vanilla extract
1 ripe mango, peeled, pitted, and diced

1. Preheat oven to 325°F.

2. Heat the almond milk and honey in a small saucepan over medium heat and bring it to a simmer.

3. Remove the saucepan from the heat.

4. In a large bowl, whisk together the eggs and vanilla until combined well.

5. Slowly add the hot milk to the egg mixture, whisking constantly.

6. Evenly divide the mango among each of 6 ramekins.

7. Pour the egg mixture over the mango. Place the ramekins in a baking dish.

8. Fill the baking dish with hot water until it comes about 1 inch up the sides of the ramekins.

9. Place the baking dish in the preheated oven and cook for about 45 minutes, until the custards are set.

10. Refrigerate the ramekins until the custards are completely cool. Serve chilled.

Slow-Cooked Carrot Pudding

Old-fashioned baked or steamed puddings were often the centerpiece of celebrations at the turn of the past century, and this simple, spicy, tasty slow-cooker creation would have fit in nicely. You can incorporate a couple of grated parsnips or a sweet potato as well in this recipe. Sprinkle a few toasted almonds or pecans on top for a little crunch.

1 tablespoon coconut oil

6 large carrots, peeled, and coarsely grated

1 teaspoon ground cinnamon

½ teaspoon sea salt

½ teaspoon ground nutmeg

¼ teaspoon allspice

½ cup maple syrup

1 cup unsweetened almond milk

4 large eggs, beaten

1. Lightly grease a slow cooker with the coconut oil.

2. In a large bowl, mix together all of the ingredients until well combined.

3. Transfer the mixture to the prepared slow cooker.

4. Cover and cook on high heat for 3 to 4 hours. Serve hot.

Decadent Chocolate Mousse

MAKES 4 SERVINGS

No one would guess that the creaminess and texture of this mousse comes from avocados. They need to be completely ripe, and peeling and pitting them does make a mess, but avocados are a great source of dietary fiber and monounsaturated fat, which can help stabilize blood sugar and protect your heart.

2 very ripe avocados, peeled and pitted
1 large ripe banana
1 cup cocoa powder
½ cup honey
½ cup toasted chopped hazelnuts

1. Place the avocados, banana, cocoa powder, and honey in a food processor and pulse until very smooth and thick.

2. Spoon into dessert bowls or fancy stemmed glasses.

3. Top the mousse with toasted hazelnuts and chill in the fridge.

4. Serve cold.

Chocolate Fondue

Fondues were the go-to dessert at parties in the 1960s, and this fun dish is making a comeback. You can dip anything Paleo friendly into the glossy chocolate sauce, but fresh fruit is particularly yummy. Homemade Paleo marshmallows, cookies, and even cake can also be festive. If your chocolate firms up too much to dip, simply melt it again on low heat.

6 ounces 72 percent dark chocolate, chopped
½ cup almond butter
Fresh fruit (bananas, peaches, oranges, strawberries, mangos) or Paleo cookies

1. Place the chocolate in a medium stainless steel bowl placed over a saucepan with gently simmering water in it over low heat.

2. Melt the chocolate and then whisk in the almond butter until very smooth.

3. Transfer the chocolate mixture to a fondue pot or serving dish.

4. Serve the chocolate and fruit with dipping forks for the chocolate.

Dark Chocolate Pots de Crème

MAKES 4 SERVINGS

"Pots de crème" is the French way of saying amazingly rich chocolate pudding. The key to this dessert is to use high-quality chocolate. Dark chocolate is a great source of antioxidants and many minerals. Eating as little as 1 ounce each day can help regulate blood sugar and support a healthy cardiovascular system.

3 large eggs

6 tablespoons honey

1½ teaspoons instant espresso powder

1½ teaspoons pure vanilla extract

6 ounces chopped unsweetened chocolate

1 cup coconut milk

2 pints fresh raspberries

1. Place the eggs, honey, espresso powder, vanilla, and chocolate in a blender and blend until smooth

2. Scald the coconut milk in a small saucepan over medium-high heat, taking care not to boil it.

3. Pour the hot coconut milk into the blender while it is running on low. Blend until the mixture is very thick and smooth.

4. Pour the chocolate mixture into serving dishes and refrigerate for at least 2 hours.

5. Top with the berries and serve.

Lime Cookies

MAKES 24 COOKIES

Sometimes all you need for dessert is a cup of coffee and a couple of truly sublime cookies. These cookies are intensely lime flavored and have a shortbread texture that melts in your mouth. Almond flour can be expensive, especially when you are using the amount called for in this recipe. The best way to create these treats in an economical manner is to make your own almond milk and save the almond meal left over after the milk is strained.

3 cups almond flour
2 teaspoons baking soda
1 teaspoon baking powder
1 tablespoon ground cinnamon
½ teaspoon sea salt
¾ cup coconut milk
⅓ cup maple syrup
2 large eggs
Juice and zest of 1 lime
1 teaspoon pure vanilla extract

1. Preheat oven to 350°F. Line two baking sheets with parchment paper.

2. In a large bowl, stir together the almond flour, baking soda, baking powder, cinnamon, and salt until well mixed.

3. In a small bowl, whisk together the remaining ingredients.

4. Add the wet ingredients to the dry ingredients and stir until blended.

5. Drop the cookie batter by the tablespoon onto the prepared baking sheets, leaving about 2 inches between cookies.

6. Bake in the preheated oven for 10 to 15 minutes, or until golden brown but still soft.

7. Cool completely.

Lemon Slices

MAKES 12 SERVINGS

These clever lemon bars will delight even hard-to-please guests. Not only are they adorable and bright, but they are also scrumptious. The lemon curd filling can be made ahead of time (and in double batches) and stored in the fridge in a sealed container.

For the crust:

2 cups almond flour

2 large eggs

½ cup coconut oil, melted

¼ cup honey

1 teaspoon pure vanilla extract

For the filling:

6 large eggs

1 cup honey

Zest of 2 lemons

Juice of 4 lemons

Pinch of sea salt

½ cup coconut oil, melted

Make the crust:

1. Preheat the oven to 325°F. Line a 9 × 13-inch baking dish with parchment paper.

2. Place the almond flour in a large bowl.

3. In a small bowl, whisk together the eggs, coconut oil, honey, and vanilla until very well combined.

4. Add the wet ingredients to the almond flour and stir until blended.

5. Press the crust mixture evenly into the prepared baking dish.

6. Bake the crust for 12 to 15 minutes, or until the edges are golden brown.

7. Set the crust aside to cool.

Make the filling:

1. Whisk together the eggs, honey, lemon zest, lemon juice, and salt in a small saucepan over medium heat until well blended.

2. Slowly whisk in the coconut oil.

3. Continue whisking until the filling thickens to a pudding-like texture.

4. Remove the filling from the heat and let it cool completely, covered with a layer of plastic wrap pressed directly onto the surface.

5. Spoon the cooled filling onto the crust and store in the freezer, wrapped with plastic wrap.

6. Remove the dessert from the freezer 30 minutes before serving, and cut into slices.

Coconut Snowballs

Coconut lovers will delight in these bite-sized treats, and they would be a lovely gift nestled in pretty paper cups placed in a charming box or basket. Coconut is a nutritional powerhouse that can improve digestion, enhance endurance, and boost energy. So enjoy this light dessert and then take an invigorating walk or even go dancing.

3 cups unsweetened shredded coconut, divided

1 tablespoon melted coconut oil

¼ cup maple syrup

3 tablespoons coconut milk

1 teaspoon pure vanilla extract

½ teaspoon ground cinnamon

Pinch of sea salt

1. Place 2 cups of the shredded coconut and the coconut oil in a food processor and pulse until it is a paste-like consistency.

2. Add all of the remaining ingredients except the remaining 1 cup coconut, and process until well mixed.

3. Add another ½ cup of the coconut to the processor and pulse until combined.

4. Roll the mixture into eighteen 1-inch balls, and then roll the balls in the remaining ½ cup of coconut.

5. Refrigerate the finished balls for a few hours to firm up. Serve cold.

Cantaloupe Granita

MAKES 4 SERVINGS

Granita, a very popular dish in Italy, is like ice cream or sorbet, but has a coarser texture. This granita is composed only of cantaloupe, honey, and a hint of salt to play up the sweetness of the melon. The trick to a perfect granita is to stir and scrape the mixture constantly throughout the process. This will ensure that you end up with the correct snowy texture that melts on the tongue rather than a solid popsicle.

1 large ripe cantaloupe, peeled, seeded, and cut into chunks
1 tablespoon honey or maple syrup
Pinch of sea salt

1. Purée the cantaloupe, honey, and salt in a food processor until very smooth and thick.

2. Transfer the purée to a sieve lined with cheesecloth and set over a large bowl. Press as much of the liquid through as possible.

3. Pour the liquid into a shallow pan and place the pan in the freezer.

4. Take the pan out of the freezer after about 30 minutes and stir it thoroughly with a spoon, taking care to scrape along the edges.

5. Place the pan back in the freezer.

6. Repeat this process until the granita begins to harden, scraping the mixture every 30 minutes until the entire mixture is a snowlike consistency. Serve frozen in martini glasses or custard cups.

Coconut Sorbet

MAKES 6 SERVINGS

This rich, creamy dessert is designed for real coconut lovers. Blending the coconut meat to a smooth mixture takes about 15 minutes in the blender, so be patient. For a truly decadent treat, try this sorbet topped with fresh pineapple chunks, sliced banana, a drizzle of dark chocolate, or a sprinkling of toasted shredded coconut. Young coconuts are different from the brown, fuzzy ripe coconuts (see page 261).

2 young coconuts, meat only
2 cups full-fat coconut milk
¼ cup honey, or to taste

1. Place the coconut meat and coconut milk in a high-speed blender and process until very smooth.

2. Add the honey by the tablespoon, pulsing after each addition, until the desired sweetness is reached.

3. Pass the coconut mixture through a fine sieve and freeze in an ice-cream maker according to the manufacturer's directions. Serve frozen.

Pineapple Gelato

Pineapple freezes beautifully, so it is a perfect choice for this sweet gelato. In the United States, gelati are similar to ice cream and are made with milk or cream, sweeteners, and fruit purées, while in Italy they are more like sorbets. This gelato lands somewhere in the middle, with very little fat and sweetener in it. If your pineapple is not very ripe, reduce the amount of lemon juice in the mixture and add a bit more maple syrup. Although pineapple is considered to be one of the sweeter fruits, it can be extremely tart when a little green, so pick your fruit carefully for the best results.

6 cups chopped ripe pineapple

½ cup unsweetened almond milk

½ cup maple syrup

1 teaspoon fresh lemon juice

1 vanilla bean, split, and seeds scraped out

246

1. Place all the ingredients in a food processor and process until very smooth.

2. Transfer the mixture to an ice-cream maker and freeze according to manufacturer's directions.

3. Serve frozen.

Strawberry Ice Cream

This is the purest strawberry ice cream you can get, with a creamy, pleasing texture and strong berry taste. The ripeness of the berries will determine the sweetness, so if they are still a little tart, add some honey while puréeing the mixture.

3 medium ripe bananas
1 cup unsweetened almond milk
4 cups strawberries, washed and trimmed

1. Place the bananas and almond milk in a food processor and pulse until smooth.

2. Add the strawberries and pulse until the strawberries are almost puréed.

3. Transfer the mixture to an ice cream maker and freeze according to the manufacturer's directions.

Apple Crumble

MAKES 8 SERVINGS

The entire house will be filled with the scent of apples, nuts, and spices when you make this delicious dessert. Maple syrup is the sweetener used, and you might not know that it comes in grades. The United States uses two grades, A and B, but Canadian maple syrup comes in three grades and up to five color classes, so read the labels to see what type appeals to you. Grade B and darker syrups are best for baking because they have a richer maple taste.

6 to 8 large tart apples, peeled and chopped

½ cup maple syrup, divided

1 tablespoon ground cinnamon

½ teaspoon ground nutmeg

¼ teaspoon ground ginger

Pinch of cloves

Pinch of sea salt

1½ cups finely chopped pecans

4 tablespoons coconut oil

1. Preheat oven to 400°F.

2. Toss the apples with ¼ cup of the maple syrup, the cinnamon, nutmeg, ginger, cloves, and salt until well mixed.

3. Transfer the apple mixture to a 9 × 13-inch baking pan.

4. In a small bowl, mix together the pecans and coconut oil until the mixture resembles coarse crumbs.

5. Add the remaining ½ cup maple syrup and stir to combine.

6. Scatter the crumble mixture evenly over the apples and bake for 30 minutes, or until the apples are fork-tender. Serve hot.

Pecan Pie

MAKES 8 SERVINGS

You might have thought pecan pie was not a Paleo-friendly dish, but this version definitely meets the requirements. The crust might become a family favorite because it tastes incredible and can work well in other pies. The pecans have more antioxidants than any other nut, which means they can fight against cell damage and cut your risk of many serious diseases such as cancer and Parkinson's.

For the crust:

1½ cups fine almond meal

¼ cup coconut oil

¼ cup honey

1 teaspoon pure vanilla extract

Pinch of sea salt

For the filling:

1 cup dates, pitted, soaked in warm water, and drained

2 cups pecans, divided

¼ cup chia seeds

1 large ripe banana

1 tablespoon pure vanilla extract

2 teaspoons ground cinnamon

Make the crust:

1. Place all the crust ingredients in a food processor and pulse until the mixture is dough-like.

2. Press the crust evenly into an 8-inch springform pan.

Make the filling:

1. Place all the filling ingredients except 1 cup of the pecans into a food processor and pulse until smooth.

2. Pour the filling evenly over crust.

3. Top the filling with the remaining 1 cup pecans.

4. Cover the pie with plastic wrap and place it in the freezer for at least 4 hours.

5. Remove the pie from the springform pan, cut, and serve.

Rich Chocolate-Banana Pie

MAKES 8 SERVINGS

This pie can be served in very thin slices because it is sweet, rich, and chocolaty. If you serve it with a scoop of fresh strawberry ice cream, you might feel as if you're eating a banana split. Keep it in the freezer to firm up completely.

For the crust:

1½ cups almond flour

6 Medjool dates, pitted and finely chopped

Pinch of sea salt

¼ cup coconut oil or as needed, and more for greasing the pie plate

For the filling:

4 large ripe bananas, cut into chunks

6 Medjool dates, pitted and chopped

1 cup unsweetened coconut milk

½ cup cocoa powder

2 teaspoons pure vanilla extract

3 ounces dark chocolate, shaved into curls with a vegetable peeler, for serving

Make the crust:

1. Preheat oven to 350°F. Lightly grease a 9-inch pie plate with coconut oil.

2. Pulse the almond flour, dates, and salt in a food processor until well mixed.

3. Add the coconut oil and pulse until the dough starts to come together in a ball. Press the dough evenly into the pie plate.

4. Bake the crust for about 15 minutes or until lightly browned and let it cool completely.

Make the filling:

1. Place all the ingredients except the dark chocolate curls, in a food processor and process until the mixture is very smooth.

2. Spoon the banana mixture into the cooled crust and top with the chocolate curls.

3. Cover the pie with plastic wrap and place in the freezer for 4 to 6 hours.

4. Take the pie out of the freezer about 30 minutes before serving.

Apple Pie Cupcakes with Spiced Frosting

MAKES 12 CUPCAKES

Cupcakes are happy food, especially if you serve them in colorful paper liners and pipe the frosting into luscious swirls. The best way to get an intense apple flavor in these cupcakes is to use homemade applesauce puréed with a couple of dried apple pieces until smooth. If you buy commercial applesauce, make sure it is organic and unsweetened so you can serve this dessert confidently and proudly to guests.

For the cupcakes:

1⅓ cups almond meal

½ cup coconut flour

1 teaspoon arrowroot starch

½ teaspoon sea salt

6 medium eggs, at room temperature

½ cup unsweetened applesauce

½ cup maple syrup

⅓ cup coconut oil, melted

For the frosting:

1 cup coconut oil

¼ cup honey

1 tablespoon ground cinnamon

Pinch of sea salt

Make the cupcakes:

1. Preheat the oven to 350°F. Line a 12-cup muffin tin with paper baking cups.

2. In a medium bowl, stir together the almond meal, coconut flour, arrowroot starch, and salt until well combined.

3. In a large bowl, beat together the eggs, applesauce, maple syrup, and coconut oil until well blended.

4. Add the dry ingredients to the wet ingredients and beat until the batter is blended.

5. Spoon the batter into the lined muffin cups so they are about three-quarters full.

continued ▶

6. Bake in the preheated oven for 25 to 30 minutes or until a toothpick inserted in the center comes out clean. Cool completely.

Make the frosting:

1. Beat all of the ingredients together a medium bowl with an electric mixer on medium speed until well combined.

2. Frost the cupcakes and serve.

Coffee Streusel Cake

MAKES 4 SERVINGS

Ribbons of cinnamon run through this buttery-tasting cake. You can dress it up easily with toasted nuts, coconut, and even a cup of raisins. If you want the streusel ribbons to be more prominent, simply make double the amount and layer it three times through the batter.

For the cake:

¼ cup coconut oil, melted, plus more for greasing the pan

4 large eggs, lightly beaten

½ cup unsweetened almond milk

½ cup honey

1 cup almond flour

¾ cup sifted coconut flour

1 tablespoon baking powder

⅛ teaspoon sea salt

For the streusel:

1 cup chopped almonds

¼ cup coconut oil

4 teaspoons honey

1 tablespoon ground cinnamon

1 teaspoon coconut flour

Make the cake:

1. Preheat oven to 350°F. Lightly grease an 8 × 8-inch baking pan with coconut oil.

2. In a large bowl, stir together the eggs, almond milk, honey, and coconut oil until well combined.

3. In a small bowl, stir together the almond flour, coconut flour, baking powder, and salt.

4. Add the dry ingredients to the wet ingredients and stir until combined.

5. Spoon half of the batter into the prepared baking pan and spread it out evenly.

Make the streusel:

1. Combine all the ingredients in a small bowl until it resembles crumbs.

2. Sprinkle half of the streusel mixture over the batter in the baking pan.

3. Spoon the rest of the coffee cake batter on top of the streusel layer, and sprinkle the top with the remaining streusel.

4. Bake the cake in the preheated oven for 30 to 35 minutes, or until a toothpick inserted in the center comes out clean. Serve warm or at room temperature.

Creamy Cheesecake

Most people think of brown fibrous coconuts when they need coconuts for a recipe. Young coconuts look completely different. They are usually green, have very little husk, and are filled with clear potassium-rich coconut water, which is wonderful in recipes. Most Asian markets and some other markets carry this type of coconut.

For the crust:

2 cups raw hazelnuts

1 cup dates, pitted

1 tablespoon apple juice

Pinch of sea salt

For the filling:

Meat of 2 young coconuts

2 cups raw cashews, soaked at least 6 hours and drained

1 cup coconut milk

Juice of 3 large lemons, about ¾ cup

½ cup almond butter

¼ to ½ cup honey

Make the crust:

1. Place the nuts in a food processor and pulse until very fine. Do not overblend.

2. Add the dates and purée until the mixture starts to ball up.

3. Add the apple juice and salt and pulse until it forms a thick dough.

4. Press the crust on the bottom and sides of an 8-inch springform pan. Set aside.

Make the filling:

1. Place all of the ingredients except the honey in a food processor and purée until the filling is very smooth and thick.

2. Add the honey, a bit at a time, until you achieve the desired sweetness.

3. Spoon the filling into the crust and refrigerate until firm, at least 6 hours.

4. Serve slices plain or with fresh fruit.

Chocolate Snack Cake

MAKES 12 SERVINGS

Snack cake sounds very casual, but this recipe is quite elegant and boasts a glorious chocolate flavor. The coffee accents and complements the chocolate, while the dates add bulk and sweetness. Medjool are the king of dates, very large and soft with a distinct caramel taste. If you have to use other dates instead, add 1 or 2 tablespoons of honey or maple syrup to the batter.

Coconut oil for greasing the baking pan
15 Medjool dates, pitted
2 small ripe bananas
5 large eggs
¾ cup coconut oil
¾ cup strong brewed coffee
1 tablespoon pure vanilla extract
¾ cup coconut flour
¾ cup cocoa powder
1½ teaspoons baking soda
½ teaspoon sea salt

1. Preheat the oven to 375°F. Lightly grease a 9 × 13-inch baking pan with coconut oil.

2. Pulse the dates in a food processor until completely smooth.

3. Add the bananas and pulse until completely combined.

4. Transfer the date mixture to a large bowl and add the eggs, coconut oil, coffee, and vanilla. Beat with an electric mixer until well mixed.

5. In a medium bowl, stir together the coconut flour, cocoa, baking soda, and salt until very well mixed.

6. Add the dry ingredients to the wet ingredients, mixing on low speed until blended, scraping down the sides of the bowl frequently.

7. Spoon the batter into the prepared pan and smooth the top with the back of a spoon.

8. Bake for 30 to 35 minutes, or until a toothpick inserted in the middle comes out clean.

9. Cool and serve.

Molten Chocolate Lava Cake

MAKES 6 SERVINGS

What could be better than this tender chocolate cake oozing with rich chocolate sauce? They are very easy to make. You can serve them either in the ramekins or pop them out onto serving plates for a more elegant presentation. Garnish with fresh berries and mint. If using ramekins, lightly grease them with oil and dust with cocoa powder so the cakes don't stick.

Coconut oil for greasing the ramekins
5 ounces dark chocolate
5 tablespoons coconut oil
2 extra-large eggs
1 teaspoon pure vanilla extract
2 tablespoons maple syrup
Pinch of sea salt
2 teaspoons cocoa powder
1 teaspoon coconut flour

1. Preheat oven to 375°F. Lightly grease six 6-ounce ramekins with coconut oil.

2. Melt the chocolate and coconut oil carefully in the microwave until smooth, taking care not to burn it. Transfer to a medium bowl and cool for 15 minutes.

3. Whisk together the eggs, vanilla, maple syrup, and salt until light and frothy.

4. Add the egg mixture to the chocolate along with the cocoa and coconut flour. Fold to incorporate all the ingredients well.

5. Spoon the batter into the prepared ramekins so they are about half full.

6. Transfer the ramekins to a baking sheet and bake for 12 to15 minutes, until the edges are set, but the center is still soft.

7. Serve warm.

Chocolate Mug Cake

MAKES 4 SERVINGS

This charming, easy-to-prepare dessert is served in the mug you cook it in and is ready in about 5 minutes, so indulging your chocolate craving is a snap. These tasty cakes are good hot or cold, so make them in advance if you are pressed for time. Make sure the mugs you use are microwave safe, because some earthenware should not be used in the microwave.

3 large ripe bananas, mashed smooth
4 large eggs
½ cup cocoa powder
5 tablespoons almond butter

1. In a large bowl, whisk together the bananas, eggs, cocoa powder, and almond butter until smooth.

2. Transfer the batter into 4 coffee mugs, filling each about two-thirds full.

3. Microwave the mugs one at a time on high for 2 ½ minutes, or until the center is set.

4. Carefully remove the mug from the microwave and serve.

Glossary

Allergen: Something that produces an immune reaction.

Blood glucose: The sugar level in blood.

Celiac disease: An autoimmune disorder that occurs from a reaction to a gluten protein (gliadin).

Cocoa powder: The powder produced after cacao nibs are ground, the cocoa butter is extracted, and the leftover brown paste is dried and ground again.

Coconut water: The clear, nutrient-packed water found in young coconuts.

Coconut butter: The meat and oil of the coconut puréed into a smooth butter.

Coconut oil: The oil that is extracted from the meat of the coconut using a centrifuge.

Coconuts: Mature coconuts contain the hard-husked, white-fleshed ripe fruit of the coconut palm. Young coconuts are softer in the earlier stages of development with no hard husk. The nutritious water they contain makes a great dairy substitute.

Crossfit: A fitness program that focuses on "constantly varied, high-intensity, functional movement," which promotes and has officially adopted the Paleo diet.

Flaxseed: The seeds from the flax plant, which are very high in many nutrients. Flaxseed can also be sprouted or ground up.

Ghee: A clarified butter that has the milk solids (lactose) removed by heating the butter.

Gluten: A protein found mostly in cereal grains. Proponents of the Paleo diet believe that people are not genetically adapted to handle gluten, which is the reason so many people have been diagnosed with celiac disease.

Glycemic index: A measurement concerning the speed with which blood sugar levels rise after eating a particular food.

Glycemic load: A rank given to foods that reflects the carbohydrate content based on the food's glycemic index.

Grass-fed meat: Meat produced from animals that are allowed to graze rather than raised in factories.

Green smoothie: A tasty blended beverage made from green leafy vegetables combined with fruit.

Ketosis: A state in which the body metabolizes protein and fat to create fuel bodies called ketones. This state occurs when there is no sugar-based fuel in the body and is often the result of an extended low-carbohydrate diet.

Lactose: A sugar found in milk that is an allergen and digestive irritant to many people.

Macronutrients: Nutrients that are required in large quantities by the body to perform its essential tasks and make up the main part of the human diet. The three macronutrients are protein, fat, and carbohydrates.

Micronutrients: Nutrients that are required in small quantities, which include vitamins, minerals, and trace minerals.

Nori: An edible seaweed.

Nutritional yeast: A nutritional supplement used as a protein source and as a substitute for cheese in vegan and raw cuisine.

Omega ratio: The ratio between omega-3 fatty acids and omega-6 fatty acids. This ratio should either be balanced or there should be more omega-3 fatty acids.

Omega-3 fatty acid: A group of three fats that are essential for good health but are not synthesized by the body (ALA, EPA, and DHA).

Omega-6 fatty acid: Unsaturated fatty acids, such as linoleic and arachidonic acid, that are considered essential but are not synthesized by the body.

Pasture-raised poultry: Fowl that have been raised in natural conditions rather than a factory setting.

Phytic acid: An anti-nutrient that can be found in most grains that prevents the absorption of nutrients in the body.

Probiotics: Live bacteria that are thought to positively impact the digestive system and help eliminate the pathogenic bacteria that can lie dormant in the body.

RDA: The recommended daily allowance of nutritional components such as vitamins and minerals.

SAD: The standard American diet.

Sea salt: A natural and unrefined salt that is considered to be healthier than processed salts.

Tahini: A tasty paste made from ground sesame seeds used in many Middle Eastern dishes.

Vanilla beans: Fragrant beans with seeds produced by the vanilla orchid on its vines.

Wakame: An edible kelp.

The Nutritional Value
of Paleo Foods

Here are some great sources of important nutrients in Paleo foods. Try to get a variety of foods every day to make sure you have a balanced diet with healthy levels of every nutrient.

Calcium: Dark leafy greens, spices, bok choy, egg yolks, almonds, sesame seeds, broccoli, figs, garlic, seafood, white fish, and some fresh herbs

Choline (vitamin B complex): Liver, eggs, beef, salmon, pork, fish, and seeds

Chromium: meats, poultry, and fish

Copper: Meats, organ meats, seafood, nuts, seeds, spices, dark chocolate, and sun-dried tomatoes

Essential fatty acids: Oily fish, dark leafy green vegetables, broccoli, walnuts, sprouted radish seeds, and squash

Fat: Olive oil, coconut oil, avocado, grass-fed butter, palm oil, lard, sesame seed oil, nuts, and seeds

Fiber: Fruits, vegetables, nuts, spices, cocoa, seeds, and dark chocolate

Fluoride: Some fish, raisins

Folic acid (folate): Dark leafy green vegetables, asparagus, avocado, sunflower seeds, eggs, oranges, and seaweed

Iodine: Iodized salt, seafood

Iron: Beef, eggs, spices, herbs, clams, mushrooms, dark chocolate, sun-dried tomatoes, and fish

Magnesium: Green leafy vegetables, nuts, seeds, halibut, quinoa, spices, artichokes, pumpkin, squash, bananas, herbs, and cocoa

Manganese: Nuts, spices, maple syrup, seeds, dark chocolate, and garlic

Phosphorus: Meat, eggs, fish, seeds, and nuts

Potassium: Sweet potato, dates, beet greens, bananas, tuna, spices, sun-dried tomatoes, egg whites, raisins, and seeds

Protein: Meats, eggs, fish, seeds, poultry, spices, dried fruits, broccoli, carrots, garlic, grape leaves, portobello mushrooms, Brussels sprouts, and nuts

Selenium: Turkey, organ meats, meats, eggs, seafood, and nuts

Sodium: Foods with added sodium chloride such as nuts, tamari sauce, and sun-dried tomatoes

Vitamin A: Sweet potato with peel, carrots, spinach, fish oil, organ meats, lamb, beef, poultry, dark leafy greens, chili powder, cantaloupe, and squash

Vitamin B1 (thiamin): Seeds, nuts, pork, lamb, some fish, and sun-dried tomatoes

Vitamin B2 (riboflavin): Lamb, pork, beef, egg, poultry, seafood, fish, and seaweed

Vitamin B3 (niacin): Meat, fish, poultry, seeds, sun-dried tomatoes, and hot peppers

Vitamin B5 (pantothenic acid): Chicken, beef, tomatoes, pork, egg, seeds, mushrooms, and avocado

Vitamin B6: Organ meats, nuts, seeds, beef, poultry, lamb, fish, and eggs

Vitamin B7 (biotin): Liver, fruits, and meats

Vitamin B12 (cobalamin): Fish, poultry, and meats

Vitamin C: Guava, peppers, kiwis, citrus fruit, strawberries, broccoli, currants, herbs, cauliflower, dark leafy greens, papaya, pineapple, and cabbage

Vitamin D: Fish liver oils, eggs, mushrooms, and fatty fish

Vitamin E: Olive oil, sunflower seeds, eggs, avocados, nuts, fish, seafood, and meats

Vitamin K: Nuts, kiwis, spinach, collard greens, broccoli, Brussels sprouts, cabbage, pomegranates, leeks, sun-dried tomatoes, asparagus, rhubarb, and celery

Zinc: Meats, some seafood, oysters, seeds, nuts, chard, pumpkin, avocados, bananas, maple syrup, eggs, and figs

Your Paleo Shopping List

The following list presents Paleo diet foods. It is not comprehensive. To help guide you, there is a list of items that should not make it into your shopping cart at the bottom of the list. Your goal is to eat 80 to 85 percent Paleo-friendly foods, so choose as many as you like from the approved list and enjoy.

Fish and Seafood

- Bass
- Clams
- Crab
- Crawfish
- Halibut
- Lobster
- Mackerel
- Oysters
- Pickerel
- Red snapper

- Salmon
- Scallops
- Shark
- Shrimp
- Sole
- Swordfish
- Tilapia
- Trout
- Tuna

Fruits

- Apples
- Apricots
- Avocados
- Bananas
- Berries

- Cherries
- Citrus fruits
- Cocoa
- Dark chocolate
- Figs

- Grapes
- Kiwis
- Mangos
- Melons
- Papayas
- Peaches
- Pineapple
- Plums
- Pomegranates
- Rhubarb
- Spices
- Tomatoes

Meats

- Beef
- Eggs
- Emu and ostrich
- Goat
- Lamb
- Other exotic meats (alligator, kangaroo, bear, reindeer, etc.)
- Poultry (chicken, turkey, goose, duck, Cornish hen)
- Pork (including nitrate-free bacon)
- Veal
- Wild game (venison, elk, buffalo, bison, rabbit)

Nuts and Seeds

- Almonds
- Cashews
- Flaxseed
- Hazelnuts
- Macadamia nuts
- Pecans
- Pine nuts
- Pumpkin seeds
- Sesame seeds
- Sunflower seeds
- Walnuts

Oils and Fats

- Avocado oil
- Coconut oil
- Ghee
- Grass-fed butter
- Hazelnut oil
- Lard
- Olive oil
- Palm oil
- Pistachio oil
- Sesame seed oil

Vegetables

- Artichoke hearts
- Asparagus
- Bean sprouts
- Beets
- Broccoli
- Brussels sprouts
- Cabbage
- Cauliflower
- Carrots
- Celery
- Cucumber
- Eggplant
- Garlic
- Green onions
- Herbs and spices
- Jicama
- Lettuce
- Mushrooms
- Onions
- Peppers
- Pumpkin
- Radishes
- Seaweed
- Snow peas
- Spinach and other dark leafy greens
- Squash
- Sweet potato
- Zucchini

Non-Paleo items that should not be on your shopping list

- Alcoholic beverages (allowed in extreme moderation)
- Dairy in any form
- Fatty meats
- Grains in any form
- Legumes (includes peanuts)
- Potatoes
- Processed foods
- Processed meats
- Soft drinks and energy drinks
- Soy products
- Sweetened fruit juices
- Sweeteners (excluding maple syrup and honey)

References

About Chronic Kidney Disease. 2013. http://www.kidney.org/kidneydisease/aboutckd.cfm.

Alwan, Dr. Ala. 2010. *Global status report on noncommunicable diseases 2010.* http://www.who.int/nmh/publications/ncd_report_full_en.pdf.

C. A. Maglione-Garves, L. Kravitz, and S. Schneider. 2005. "Cortisol connection: Tips on managing stress and weight." *ACSM's Health & Fitness Journal*: 20–23.

CDC/National Center for Health Statistics. 2013. *Leading Causes of Death.* January 11. http://www.cdc.gov/nchs/fastats/lcod.htm.

Colten, H. R., and B. M. Altevogt. 2006. "Extent and Health Consequences of Chronic Sleep Loss and Sleep Disorders." In *Sleep Disorders and Sleep Deprivation: An Unmet Public Health Problem.* Washington, D.C.: National Academies Press (US).

Cordain, Loren, et al. 2005. "Origins and evolution of the Western diet: Health implications for the 21st century:1,2." *The American Journal of Clinical Nutrition*: 341–354.
"Dr. Loren Cordain." 2010. *The Paleo Diet.* http://thepaleodiet.com/dr-loren-cordain/.

Fallon, Sally. 2011. "Dirty Secrets of the Food Processing Industry." *Weston A. Price.* March. http://www.westonaprice.org/modern-foods/dirty-secrets-of-the-food-processing-industry.

Farrell, Richard J., and Ciaran P. Kelley. 2002. "Celiac Sprue." *New England Journal of Medicine*: 180–188.

Frassetto, L. A., et al. 2009. "Metabolic and physiologic improvements from consuming a Paleolithic, hunter-gatherer type diet." *European Journal of Clinical Nutrition.*

Gadsby, Patricia, and Leon Steele. (October) 2004. "The Inuit Paradox: How can people who gorge on fat and rarely see a vegetable be healthier than we are?" *Discover.*

Heiden, Matthew, G. Vander, Lewis C. Cantley, and Craig B. Thompson. 2011. "Understanding the Warburg Effect: The Metabolic Requirements of Cell Proliferation." *Science*: 1029–1033.

Hermann, Janice R. 2013. "Protein and the Body." *Oklahoma State University.* http://pods.dasnr.okstate.edu/docushare/dsweb/Get/Document-2473/T-3163web.pdf.

Hu, Sanjay, R. Patel, and Frank B. 2008. "Short sleep duration and weight gain: A systematic review." *Obesity*: 643–653.

Jönsson, Tommy, et al. 2005. "Agrarian Diet and Diseases of Affluence: Do evolutionary novel diet lectins cause lectin resistance?" *BMC Endocrine Disorders*.

Kravitz, L., and R. Vaughan. 2013. "Carbohydrate intake for endurance training: Redefining traditional views." *IDEA Fitness Journal*: 20–22.

Lectins in Dry Legumes. (September 21) 2011. http://www.hc-sc.gc.ca/fn-an/securit/chem-chim/toxin-natur/lectin-legum-eng.php.

Ludvigsson, J .F., et al. 2009. "Small intestinal histopathy and mortality risk in celiac disease." *The Journal of the American Medical Association*: 1171–8.

Mayo Clinic staff. *Metabolic Syndrome*. (April 5) 2013. http://www.mayoclinic.com/health/metabolic%20syndrome/DS00522.

Study shows metabolic adaptation in calorie restriction - See more at: http://www.nia.nih. gov/nStudy Shows Metabolic Adaption in Calorie Restriction. 06 26, 2013. Study shows metabolic adaptation in calorie restriction - See more at: http://www.nia.nih.gov/newsroom/announcements/2009/05/study-shows-metabolic-adaptation-calorie-restriction#sthash. t9QVI3gm.dpuf.

Mitchell, P. C., and R. W. Welch. "Food processing: A century of change." *BMB Oxford Journals*. http://bmb.oxfordjournals.org/content/56/1/1.2.full.pdf.

Prenatal Nutrition. February 10, 2011. http://www.hc-sc.gc.ca/fn-an/nutrition/prenatal/index-eng.php.

"Protein: Moving Closer to Center Stage." *Harvard School of Public Health*. 2009. http://www.hsph.harvard.edu/nutritionsource/protein-full-story/.

Redman, L. M. et al..2009. "Metabolic and behavioral compensations in response to caloric restriction: Implications for the maintenance of weight loss." *Plos ONE*.

Ryan, Denise. *Study shows dramatic link between cancer, high-carb diets*. (June 6) 2011. http://www.vancouversun.com/health/empowered-health/Study+shows+dramatic+link+between+cancer+high+carb+diets/4946728/story.html.

Sohal, Rajindar S., and Richard Weindruch. 1996. "Oxidative Stress, Caloric Restriction, and Aging." *Science*: 59–63.

World Health Organization. 2005. *Rethinking "diseases of affluence": The economic impact of chronic diseases*. http://www.who.int/chp/chronic_disease_report/media/Factsheet4.pdf.

Index

Index

Index

Index

Index

Index